S

# Miniature ponds

WALTER SCHIMANA

MURDOCH
BOOKS

# Introduction and contents

## A miniature water world

Just because you do not have a garden big enough for a pond does not mean that you have to forego the pleasure of having a water garden. Both balcony and patio can be designed to create variety and interest by installing mini ponds featuring attractive water plants, so that you will be able to sit and enjoy the calming effect of water.

In this *Success With* Guide, Walter Schimana, a gardener with decades of experience in the design and creation of water gardens, will show you the right way to build a mini pond, what plants to use, and how to look after them. He will supply advice and tips on how to realize your own ideas and preferences. You will find out exactly how to plant which kinds of plants in basins, containers and troughs, and how to combine and supplement the plants decoratively. You will also find a host of stimulating tips for the design of pleasant seating areas. The many atmospheric photos included in this book show a whole range of design examples, along with precise instructions for DIY building, installing, care and overwintering your mini ponds. The author and the *Success With* series editing team wish you success and enjoyment with the installation and design of your miniature pond.

*Mini pond with mare's tail and rushes.*

*Shallow water water-lily*

*Iris*

### The author
Walter Schimana has been running a garden centre specializing in herbaceous plants, water plants and pond design for over 30 years. He has written several reference books on the subjects of herbaceous plants and water gardens and, since 1980, has been the consultant for the use of herbaceous plants, water plants and water gardens at the 'Bildungsstätte des Deutschen Gartenbaus' (German Education Centre for Garden Design).

### The photographers
Friedrich Strauss is a diploma garden design engineer. He followed his training in garden design with a study of art history. He has been supplying photographs to well-known garden specialist periodicals and publishers of garden books for many years. Many other photos are by well-known plant photographers (see credits, page 62).

### The illustrator
Renate Holzner works as a freelance illustrator and graphic artist for well-known publishers and agencies. Her repertoire ranges from line drawings through photo-realistic illustrations to computer graphics.

### Important:
Please read the Author's Notes on page 63, so that your enjoyment of your mini pond is not impaired.

# Layout and planting

Water combined with some fascinating water plants can create an enchanted realm on your balcony or patio. Even here, a mini pond will enable you to recreate a piece of nature. To be successful, you should plan the layout exactly, thoroughly check the characteristics of the location and carefully choose the plants for this small biotope.

*Top: Terracotta bowl with water lettuce and bog bean.*
*Left: The combination makes all the difference – purple loosestrife, sweet galingale, iris, bamboo and water crowfoot go well together.*

# Planning and preparing

## A small water paradise beside your house

Balconies, loggias or patios can be seen as an outside extension of the living area and enhance the quality of your home, as they invite you to spend your leisure time in them. In the past, balcony areas were often framed by the obligatory flowerboxes attached to a railing or balustrade but, nowadays, more variety is sought when designing these open areas. Plant troughs or containers with bushes and small trees, flowering herbaceous plants or climbing plants have transformed balconies and patios into green oases – there are no longer any limits to the wealth of ideas for planting.

Water features have been popular for ages – often in the shape of a garden pond or a stream; but, increasingly, this element of garden design has been gaining acceptance for areas nearer the house. Garden enthusiasts without a garden need not be left out: they can create beautiful water gardens in a relatively small area, even in the most cramped of spaces. Naturally, conditions will be rather different in smaller areas than in the garden, when you are planning to install containers with large areas of water. You will only be successful and achieve the result you were hoping for if you carefully consider all the questions involved with this kind of installation.

## What is a miniature pond?

As the name implies, we are dealing with plants in a small to extremely restricted area, in which water is the predominant element. Water has to be contained in vessels for this purpose. The mini water garden might, therefore, be only a small container – for example, a basin or a flower box – in which individual plants can unfold their full beauty during the course of the year. But it might also consist of a grouping of several different-sized troughs, that can be combined with each other (see page 46). A mini landscape with a water surface, water plants and surrounding plantings has a special appeal, and cannot, of course, be achieved in smaller containers, but will require the use of larger troughs (see pages 36–7).

## Designing with mini ponds

A mini pond can fulfill various aesthetic functions on a balcony, a roof garden or a loggia. This applies particularly when it is combined with other plants that also grow in the containers or troughs.

Bushes or small trees in containers may help to provide visual screens or windbreaks. Several mini ponds can be placed in front of or between them. Flat dishes or basins full of flowering plants will provide additional splashes of colour. With appropriate placing, even big roof gardens or larger balconies can be divided up into smaller, more intimate areas. Mini water gardens on balustrades, in combination with other plants in troughs – like herbaceous plants, small bushes or summer flowers – will provide a collection of attractive plants of ongoing variety and colour all year round.

## Timetable and choice of position

Once you have decided on the layout for a mini pond, you should allow sufficient time for the detailed planning of your project. Water and marginal plants are grown in containers by specialist trading companies and nurseries. The advantage of this is that they can be replanted during the entire vegetation period, will establish themselves in mini water gardens without any problems, and will continue to grow and flourish there.

*A mini water garden may consist of a group of different-sized troughs.*

## Location and timetable

You do not, therefore, need to stick to a fixed time for the installation and planting of your mini pond. We do recommend, however, that you begin with the planning and preparation the winter before.

You should think carefully when choosing a position for your mini pond and observe the spot for a few weeks before. What are the lighting conditions like? How much sunlight is there? What are wind and temperature conditions like? (See page 9.) This will enable you to plan the required protection from sun or wind at the very start, and the choice of plants can be adapted to and determined by the local conditions.

From the end of the second month of spring, temperatures on balconies and patios will be favourable enough for freshly replanted plants to carry on growing vigorously. Planning should be finished by the first month of summer at the latest, so that you can choose from the full range of plants on offer and they will all have the maximum opportunity to establish themselves and grow well.

# Planning and preparing

## Building considerations

When planning a mini water landscape on a balcony or roof garden, it is absolutely essential to check the strength of the structures, whether they are capable of carrying the extra weight and offer suitable drainage. In the case of roof gardens, the water will flow via a gully out through drainage pipes inserted in the house wall. Balcony drainage usually takes place by means of a sloping surface to a rainwater gutter, or a water spout. Both types should be checked and cleaned out several times a year.

*The weight-bearing capacity of the ground or floor must be checked for heavy containers.*

## Weight-bearing capacity

It is essential to consider the fact that the added weight of several large plant troughs will not have been calculated in the original builders' plans. In general, you can assume that a weight limit need not be applied if your troughs are standing close to the outer walls of the building. In the case of a large roof garden that is to be divided by groups of mini ponds and other plant containers, you should ensure that weight-bearing walls are underneath or close to them. As even builders' plans do not always supply reliable information on these matters, it is recommended that you obtain additional information from the architect or from a structural engineer. In the case of free-hanging balconies that have no support at the front edge, you should not place larger troughs in the front section. Usually, there should be no problem with positions close to the outer wall.

## Calculating the weight

The architect or structural engineer will need to see the original plans of the building (where a roof garden is concerned, the plan of the floor with the roof garden and of the floor below) so that he can give relevant advice.

To estimate the total weight of your mini pond, multiply the weight in kg of the container or trough itself plus the plants by 1.7. If you employ this formula, you should always be within the safety margin, as 1 litre of water weighs 1kg and, therefore, any heavier parts of the contents – like sand, for example, at 1.75kg per litre – will definitely be accounted for in the calculation.

### Balustrades and railings

Larger flower boxes, from 15cm (6in) high and 20cm (8in) wide, and of any length, can accommodate mini ponds very well, so the boxes can be installed on a balustrade or fixed to the railing. In general, the rule is that flower boxes should be affixed to the inside of upper-floor balconies.

### Legal questions

Basically, there should be no legal difficulties with installing mini ponds on balconies or patios, providing the installation of other types of plant troughs has been permitted. In rented apartments, mini ponds that are cemented or otherwise permanently fixed on the balcony or patio, along with water connections, should first be authorized by the landlord. In the case of owner-occupied apartments, any necessary authorization by the freeholders (if any) should be sought first. The risk of water damage is relatively low. If there are problems, it is usually due to a leaking trough that is losing water steadily but slowly. A proper drainage facility should be able to cope with this. In any case, we recommend checking with your insurers for these eventualities.

### Location

It is essential that water, clean air and light are present in sufficient measure for the plants to flourish.

*Water* A great deal of water will be lost by the mini pond due to evaporation in sun and wind. During the summer (particularly on hot days), water will have to be added regularly (see page 50). Smaller containers can be topped up with a watering can during the daily watering of plants. If you have several larger troughs, it would be best to install a tap and a hose nearby, so that water can be replenished easily.

*Light* This is one of the most important considerations for growth. The position for a mini pond should benefit from six to eight hours of sunshine daily. Naturally, there are water plants that can manage with less sunlight (see tables, pages 14-15 and 18-19) but, in principle, it is preferable to choose a lighter position. North-facing balconies, with little sunlight, are not very suitable positions.

*Temperature* Due to their exposed positions, mini water gardens on balconies and patios are strongly subject to daily and seasonal changes in temperature. The plants will cope quite well with daily fluctuations. Provided the water level is high enough, plants should not suffer from exposure to sunlight, even in temperatures around 30°C (86°F). Frost in the

autumn, winter and spring should not create problems for most indigenous water and marginal plants, provided proper overwintering preparations (see pages 54–5) have been made. Exotic, frost-sensitive species should be overwintered in frost-free conditions, so they do not die.

*Power supply* Light features and flowing water are popular additions to miniature water gardens and for these you need a power supply on your balcony or patio. The juxtaposition of water and electricity does, of course, demand special safety measures, in the form of a residual circuit breaker (see pages 42–3).

*Transportation of containers* When deciding the size of a mini pond feature, you should always consider how you will transport heavy or large troughs to their final position. It will help to move medium-sized containers if there is a lift in the building and you can gain access to the balcony or patio directly from the house.

# Planning and preparing

## Check list

**Timetable** Can the installation of the mini pond be carried out by the end of the second month of summer?
**Structure** In the case of larger troughs, check with the architect or a structural engineer, and look at builders' plans.
**Legal questions** (for tenants or owners of apartments): Has permission been granted in the tenancy agreement or lease to instal larger plant containers? For permanently fixed mini ponds you may have to seek permission from a tenancy association in the apartment block.
**Light** Are the light conditions in the chosen position sufficient for water and marginal plants (at least six hours of sunshine per day for water-lilies)?

**Water** Is a constant supply of water guaranteed, without any problems?
**Protection from sun and wind** Should protection from sun and wind be planned as part of the installation?
**Overwintering** Is a light, cool but frost-free room available for frost-sensitive species? Or will the plants have to overwinter outside (in which case, choose appropriate plants)?
**Power supply** Does the position have a power source and is it properly secured?
**Transport** Are there ways and means of transporting heavy containers to the balcony or roof garden (lift, access to patio from the apartment)?

**Important**: Do not use any freshly treated wooden containers, as the vapours will damage sensitive water plants.
**Stoneware or ceramic basins** look very attractive and are good for planting. They are watertight, but suffer from the disadvantage that they break easily and do not cope well with frost or ice. For this reason, they should be placed in a frost-free position during the winter months. Stoneware and ceramic containers are expensive (ceramic ware from Asia is cheaper), so those on a tight budget may decide to opt for cheaper, plastic imitations. These are not to everyone's taste, but can be well disguised with a beautiful and deft arrangement of plants. The advantages are much less weight, greater durability, and less damage by frost.
**Clay basins or containers** will only be suitable for mini water gardens if they are glazed on the inside at least.

If you choose unglazed clay containers, water will penetrate the pores to the outside and be lost continuously. In addition, evaporation will cause the vessel to cool down. The clay vessel will, therefore, be constantly damp and subject to weathering damage.

## Containers: an overview

If you choose smaller containers, the installation and design will be more flexible. They are more suitable for smaller balconies or a loggia. Only a large balcony or roof garden will offer appropriate space for larger, heavier, and less mobile troughs. Containers for a mini pond can be found in a great variety of materials.
**Wood** is particularly popular – the first miniature gardens in England were mostly installed in halved whiskey barrels. They are

made of oak and are, therefore, very durable and longlasting. Unfortunately, they are rarely obtainable now.

Other wooden containers, like herring barrels or wash tubs, are suitable, but they must be of very durable wood and lined with watertight material on the inside.

Wooden troughs can be bought ready assembled or can be built according to your own measurements and needs (see pages 40–1).

*Bowls and containers made of clay are very attractive, but should be glazed on the inside.*

*For stone and concrete troughs* from a certain size and weight upwards, there will be problems: firstly, during transport, then with respect to the load-bearing capacity of the position you have chosen (see page 8). Positioning several large containers will, in principle, only be an option if there is sufficient space, an architect has approved the design and the containers can be transported to their final position by a building company.

Light concrete troughs are much easier to transport and move about but will often require a coat of waterseal. You can make your own troughs out of natural stone, tiles, planks, beams or railway sleepers. Flat basins can be equipped with a frame, into which plants can be inserted.

# Planning and preparing

Good water plant and herbaceous plant nurseries generally offer some 100 to 150 different species for sale. These will mainly be hardy herbaceous plants, that either die down above ground every year and shoot again in the following spring, or are evergreen and present an attractive picture all year round. Most perennial water plants, however, have a tendency to proliferate strongly, a feature that should be considered when selecting the planting density and the size of your container. When choosing plants, we recommend considering their winter appearance too, as some non-evergreen plants retain their decorative fruit stands and leaves during the winter. For example, frog bit species, with their very graceful fruit stands, look attractive when they are covered in hoar frost or snow. The fruit capsules of the iris species and any grass species that remain upright in the pond will enliven a bare and wintery water garden.

## Submerged oxygenating plants

For the most part, these plants grow under water, but occasionally may push up leaves above the water surface or just below the surface. These species should be included in any water garden, as they have a water purifying effect, give off plenty of oxygen to the water and absorb nutrients dissolved in the water. Some of them can, however, become a nuisance, due to over-vigorous growth and should be kept to a minimum or used only in larger troughs (see table page 14).

## Surfacing plants

There are two different types. One type is rooted in the bottom and only pushes up leaves and flowers to the surface. They are planted either on the bottom of the container or inserted in a plant basket. Among this group are the water-lily species, for example. Other surfacing plants float with their leaves on the surface, but are not rooted at the bottom. Among these are frog bit (*Hydrocharis morsus-ranae*) and water hyacinth (*Eichhornia crassipes*).

## Shallow water species

Herbaceous plants that grow in the vicinity of the banks of ponds (from 5–50cm/2–20in deep water) have quite flexible requirements and will still flourish in mini water gardens, in shallow water from 5-10cm (2–4in) deep. If conditions are wet enough, shallow water plants will even grow on the upper bank or in the marginal zone, a few centimetres above the water level. Among these, however, are many of the vigorously spreading species mentioned on page 16, that are only of limited suitability for a mini pond.

## Marginal plants

The marginal zone is the area of very wet soil at the edge of the water. Plants are no longer standing completely in the water, but the base of the leaves and neck of the rootstock are above water. Almost all species in this group can stand occasional flooding, but it should not become a regular occurrence, and is practically not possible anyway in a mini pond. Here, the opposite will occasionally happen, if the water supply is interrupted and the water level sinks too low. As long as the root tips can still reach water, the marginal plants will not suffer any serious harm. Moisture-loving plants grow in areas that are situated 1–15cm (4–6in) and more above the water level. They are particularly suitable for the tub-within-tub planting (see pages 36–7).

Water-lily 'Perfecta'

Water fringe

Pickerel weed

Iris

Bog bean

Water-lily 'Lilacea'

# Unique flowering beauties

There are myriad plants that grow in and near water. With their wealth of colours and rich variety of shapes they should take a prominent position in the design and general scheme of the water garden. Water-lilies and other surfacing plants are at home in the deep zone, whereas upright growing water plants and moisture-loving plants will thrive in the marginal zone and on the bank.

# Surfacing plants

| Name | Flower | Leaf | Position | Water depth / Height of growth | Comments |
|---|---|---|---|---|---|
| dwarf water–lily *Nymphaea pygmaea* 'Graziella' | orange to yellow LSP–MA | brown on top spotted | ○ | 10–30cm (4–12in) very low | very good dwarf variety, also suitable for smallest containers |
| yellow dwarf water-lily *Nymphaea pygmaea* 'Helvola' | yellow star shape LSP–MA | brown spotted | ○ | 10–30cm (4–12in), very low | does not form rhizomes, not hardy, overwinter in frost-free place |
| red dwarf water-lily *Nymphaea pygmaea* 'Rubra' | pink to red LSP–MA | green on top, underside reddish | ○ | 10–30cm (4–12in), low | hardy, largest pygmy variety |
| white dwarf water-lily *Nymphaea tetragona* 'Alba' | pure white LSP–MA | small, green | ○ | 10–30cm (4–12in), very low | does not form rhizomes, self-sowing |
| water-lily 'Berthold' *Nymphaea* 'Berthold' | warm pink LSP–MA | young leaves spotted | ○ | 20–50cm (8–20in), low | good new variety, also for smaller containers |
| water-lily *Nymphaea carolinia* 'Perfecta' | pink star shape LSP–MA | green, large 5–20cm (2–8in) | ○ | 30–50cm (12–20in), low | flowers profusely all day, prefers a open position |
| water-lily *Nymphaea* 'Chrysantha' | yellow-apricot LSP–MA | strong brown markings | ○ | 15–30cm (6–12in), low | very attractive colour, also suitable for small containers |
| water-lily *Nymphaea laydekeri* 'Lilacea' | lilac pink LSP–MA | brown spots | ○ | 20–50cm (8–20in), low | strong scent of roses, very popular |
| water-lily *Nymphaea laydekeri* 'Purpurata' | crimson LSP–MA | dark brown markings | ○ | 20–50cm (8–20in), low | tried and tested variety, flowers profusely |
| water-lily *Nymphaea* 'Moorei' | yellow LSP–MA | brown dots | ○ | 20–30cm (8–12in), low | very healthy variety |
| water hawthorn *Aponogeton distachyos* | white spike ES–MA | 10cm (4in) long oval | ○ | 10–40cm (4–16in), low | strongly scented, not hardy, overwinter young seedlings in bright place |
| frog bit *Hydrocharis morsus-ranae* | white MS–LS | round, like a water-lily | ○ | 10–40cm (4–16in), low | indigenous, floating, axil buds overwinter on the bottom |
| water fringe *Nymphoides peltata* | yellow MS–LS | small round | ○-◑ | 20–50cm (8–20in), runners | indigenous variety, very versatile in use, robust |
| water lettuce *Pistia stratiotes* | inconspicuous | bluish to light green | ○ | 15–20cm (6–8in) | tropical plant, frost-free overwintering |

# Submerged oxygenating plants

| Name | Flower | Leaf | Position | Water depth / Height of growth | Comments |
|---|---|---|---|---|---|
| hornwort, rigid *Ceratophyllum demersum* | inconspicuous | in whorls, needle shaped | ○-◑ | 10–100cm (4–40in), no roots | indigenous, good water cleansing, overwinters as short shoot |
| stonecrop *Crassula recurva* | inconspicuous ES–MS | needle shaped 1cm (⅜in) | ○-● | 0–50cm (0–20in), very vigorous | oxygen producing, vigorous growth, limited use |
| rush *Eleocharis acicularis* | inconspicuous ES–EA | thin, grass-like | ○-◑ | 0–70cm (0–28in), carpet-like | good water cleansing, easy-going |
| water crowfoot *Ranunculus aquatilis* | white ES–MS | finely feathered | ○-◑ | 10–100cm (4–40in), medium vigorous | indigenous species, produces tri-lobed floating leaves together with flower |
| water soldier *Stratoites aloides* | white ES–MS | lancet shaped, prickly | ○-● | 20–50cm (8–20in), rosettes | indigenous species, lifts flower above water surface |
| common bladderwort *Utricularia vulgaris* | yellow ES–LS | feathery | ○ | rootless, low | has sticky bladders for catching small insects, nutrient-poor, soft water |

| Name | Flower | Leaf | Position | Water depth / Height of growth | Comments |
|---|---|---|---|---|---|
| sweet flag *Acorus calamus* | green club ES–MS | sword-shaped | ○ | 0–10cm (0–4in), 70cm (28in) | Healing plant, shoot and leaf have strong, aromatic scent |
| variegated sweet flag *Acorus calamus* 'Variegatus' | green club ES–MS | broad, white longways stripes | ○ | 0–10cm (0–4in), 70cm (28in) | grows less vigorously than the regular species |
| water plantain *Alisma plantago-aquatica* | white, filigree MS–EA | lancet-shaped, long stalk | ○-◐ | 0–40cm (0–16in), 40–100cm (16–40in) | produces lots of seed, fruit stand decorative in winter |
| narrow-leafed water plantain *Alisma lanceolata* | delicate pink ES–LS | narrow lancet shaped | ○-◐ | 0–30cm (0–12in), 20–50cm (8–20in) | little growth, suitable for small containers, ornamental |
| flowering rush *Butomus umbellatus* | pink umbels ES–LS | three-edged, grass-like | ○ | 10–50cm (4–20in), 60–100cm (24–40in) | indigenous species, varieties 'Snowhite' and 'Rose Red' |
| sweet-grass, variegated *Glyceria maxima* 'Variegata' | brownish MS | reed-like, variegated | ○ | 0–40cm (0–16in), 100–120cm (40–48in) | grows rampantly, insert within a slightly larger container |
| mare's tail *Hippuris vulgaris* | inconspicuous LSP–LS | needle-like | ○ | 10–40cm (4–16in), 30cm (12in) | medium rampant growth, plant within a container |
| iris *Iris laevigata* | white, blue, pink MS | grass-like | ○-◐ | 10cm (4in), 60–80cm (24–32in) | varieties: 'Alba' (white), 'Monstrosa' (white/blue), 'Rose Queen' (pink) |
| bog bean *Menyanthes trifoliata* | delicate pink LSP–ES | tripartite, leathery | ○-◐ | 0–30cm (0–12in), 30cm (12in) | indigenous species, creeping |
| water milfoil *Myriophyllum aquaticum* | does not flower here | finely feathered | ○-◐ | 0–40cm (0–16in), 10–15cm (4–6in) | overwinter in frost-free place, turns light green above water, very luxuriant |
| golden club *Orontium aquaticum* | yellow club LSP–ES | lancet-like blue green | ○-◐ | 10–30cm (4–12in), 20cm (8in) | forms floating leaves from 25cm (10in) deep |
| pickerel weed *Pontederia cordata* | blue spikes ES–LS | arrow-shaped, long stalk | ○ | 20–50cm (8–20in), 80–100cm (32–40in) | water, overwinter in frost-free place overwinter in container in frost-free place |
| arrowhead (double variety) *Sagittaria latifolia* 'Plena' | white pompoms panicle, LS | broad, large arrow-shaped | ○-◐ | 10–30cm (4–12in), 50–60cm (20–24in) | overwinter in frost-free place, wanders, keep in own container |
| arrowhead *Sagittaria sagittifolia* | white, violet ES–LS | narrow pointed, arrow-shaped | ○-◐ | 10–30cm (4–12in), 30–40cm (12–16in) | dainty, wanders (place within container) overwinter in frost-free place |
| bulrush *Scirpus lacustris* 'Albescens' | brown MS–LS | round, white longways stripes | ○-◐ | 10–60cm (4–24in), 100–150cm (40–60in) | very elegant, grows less vigorously than wild type |
| Zebra rush, *Scirpus lacustris Tabernaemontani* 'Zebrinus' | brown MS–LS | round, white crossways stripes | ○-◐ | 10–30cm (4–12in), 80–120cm (32–48in) | the stalks bend over easily at the white cross stripes |
| Laxmann reed mace *Typha laxmannii* | mousy, brown MS–EA | grass-like, 0.5cm (¼in) wide | ○ | 5–30cm (2–12in), 130–150cm (52–60in) | slightly rampant, keep in own container if necessary |
| grey-brown reed mace *Typha shuttleworthii* | grey brown, short MS–EA | grass-like, 1cm (¾in) wide | ○ | 5–30cm (2–12in), 120cm (48in) | keep in own container, if planted in very small containers |
| bog iris *Iris pseudacorus* | golden yellow ES–MS | sword-like | ○ | 0–30cm (0–12in), 100–120cm (40–60in) | plant individually, repot annually and divide |
| horsetail *Equisetum hiemale* 'Robustum' | no flowers | round stalk, winter green | ○-◐ | 0–30cm (0–12in), 150cm (60in) | vigorous growth, plant individually, repot annually, divide |
| sweet galingale *Cyperus longus* | greenish LSP–ES | grass-like leaf whorls. | ○ | 10–30cm (4–12in), 100cm (40in) | the long leaves of the leaf whorl will grow to 100cm (40in) |

# Planning and preparing

The different planting zones are distinguished as follows: bank or marginal zone, shallow water or shallow zone, and deep water zone. The water level for each type of planting is always determined by the size and height of the plant container. Depth of planting and planting density, as well as special needs, can be found on the plant labels, or ask a water plants expert.

**Note:** The following species are suitable only for mini ponds in larger troughs. For smaller containers, use them on their own: common flag (*Iris pseudacorus*), water parsnip (*Berula erecta*), sweet galingale (*Cyperus longus*), Canadian pondweed (*Eleodea canadensis*), horsetail (*Equisetum hiemale*), common reed (*Phragmites australis*), water crowfoot (*Ranunculus lingua*), branched bur-weed (*Sparganium erectum* and *Sparganium simplex*), reed mace (*Typha angustifolia* and *Typha latifolia*).

Purple loosestrife

Water forget-me-not

Yellow water-lily

Rush

Water crowfoot

When you observe a pond in the wild, you will be able to distinguish various plants with very different requirements in the same location. When planting species in your mini pond, you should consider their differing requirements, so that they will flourish successfully and thrive for a long time. Plants placed in the wrong zone will very rapidly disappear from the mini water garden and a gap will appear that needs to be closed.

*Mare's tail*

# Different planting zones in your miniature water garden

*Small reed mace*

*Creeping-Jenny*

# Marginal plants

| Name | Flower | Leaf | Position | Growth | Comments |
|------|--------|------|----------|--------|----------|
| broad-leafed water plantain<br>*Alisma subcordata* | delicate pink<br>ES–LS | egg-shaped,<br>green | ○ | tufty<br>1.50cm (⅗in) | very beautiful, broad leaf |
| lesser water plantain<br>*Baldellia ranunculoides* | delicate pink, small<br>ES–MA | spade-shaped<br>small | ○ | tufty<br>5–10cm (2–4in) | charming marginal plant,<br>some protection for overwintering |
| bog arum ☠<br>*Calla palustris* | white,<br>MSP–MS | heart-shaped<br>10cm (4in) | ◑ | creeping,<br>15–25cm (6–10in) | indigenous, attractive red fruit<br>stand, berries toxic! |
| marsh marigold (king cup)<br>*Caltha palustris* | yellow<br>MSP–LSP | round, long<br>stalk | ○–◑ | tufty,<br>40cm (16in) | the double variety 'Multiplex'<br>flowers longer |
| great marsh marigold<br>*Caltha palustris* 'Thyermannii' | large, yellow<br>MSP–ES | large, round | ○–◑ | horizontal,<br>40cm (16in) | horizontal shoots that form<br>roots |
| sedge<br>*Carex gravi* | green, prickly<br>MS–LS | narrow,<br>folded | ○–◑ | tufty,<br>40–50cm (16–20in) | two morning star-like fruits<br>per stalk |
| marsh spurge ☠<br>*Euphorbia palustris* | yellow umbel<br>LSP–ES | lancet-shaped,<br>autumn colours | ○–◑ | tufty,<br>50cm (20in) | yellow autumn colour with red<br>stalks. Toxic milky sap! |
| hosta<br>*Hosta* hybrid 'Golden Tiara' | purple violet<br>MS–LS | light green,<br>yellow edge | ○–● | tufty,<br>20–40cm (8–16in) | other variety: 'Halcyon'<br>(blue leafed) |
| marsh pennywort<br>Hydrocotyle novae-zelandiae | inconspicuous<br>yellowish | round,<br>blunt toothed edges | ○–◑ | creeping,<br>3cm (1⅛in) | small 'carpets', grows around larger<br>stones, needs winter protection |
| iris<br>*Iris setosa* | violet, white<br>ES | narrow,<br>grass-like | ○–◑ | tufty,<br>50cm (20in) | very robust |
| rush<br>*Juncus decipiens* 'Spiralis' | brown<br>ES–LS | dainty<br>spirally turned | ○ | tufty,<br>20cm (8in) | its dainty growth makes it suitable<br>for the smallest containers |
| soft rush<br>*Juncus effusus* 'Spiralis' | brown<br>ES–LS | round,<br>spirally turned | ○ | tufty,<br>40cm (16in) | an interesting variety of the<br>indigenous rush |
| rush<br>*Juncus ensifolius* | black brown<br>ES–LS | sword-like<br>narrow | ○–◑ | tufty,<br>20cm (8in) | forms seeds |
| creeping-Jenny<br>*Lysimachia nummularia* | yellow<br>ES–MS | round,<br>penny-sized | ○–● | creeping,<br>3cm (1⅛in) | can grow into the water,<br>variety 'Aurea' has yellow leaves |
| purple loosestrife<br>*Lythrum salicalia* | red<br>MS–LS | willow-like | ○ | tufty,<br>80–120cm (32–48in) | indigenous, good varieties:<br>'Stichflamme' and 'Zigeunerblut'<br>('Tongue of Flame' and 'Gypsy Blood') |
| loosestrife *Lythrum*<br>*virgatum* 'Rose Queen' | pinkish red<br>MS–LS | willow-like | ○ | tufty,<br>70cm (28in) | the new variety is daintier<br>'Dropmore Purple' (purple violet) |
| water forget-me-not<br>*Myosotis palustris* | blue, white rarely,<br>LSP–ES | longish oval,<br>hairy | ○–◑ | horizontal | indigenous, easily forms seed,<br>flowers anew after cutting back |
| forget-me-not<br>*Myosotis rehsteinerii* | blue<br>ES–LS | small,<br>oval | ○ | carpet-like,<br>3–5cm (1⅕–2in) | indigenous, likes slightly gravelly<br>soil, ground covering |
| drumstick primrose<br>*Primula denticulata* | blue, white, red<br>MSP | tongue-like,<br>toothed edge | ○–◑ | tufty,<br>15–20cm (6–8in) | very durable, if position constantly<br>moist |
| giant yellow cowslip<br>*Primula florindae* | yellow, bell-shaped<br>ES–MS | round, red<br>stalk | ○–◑ | tufty,<br>15–30cm (6–12in) | scented, similar species<br>*Primula sikkimensis* |
| candelabra primrose<br>*Primula japonica* | red, white<br>LSP–ES | tongue-like,<br>white nerves | ○–◑ | tufty,<br>20–40cm (8–16in) | further candelabra primrose<br>*Primula bullesiana* in many colours |

○ = sunny    ◑ = semi-shade    ● = shade    ☠ = toxic

| Name | Flower | Leaf | Growth | Comments |
|---|---|---|---|---|
| larkspur *Delphinium belladonna* 'Atlantis' | radiant blue, ES | hand-like, feathered | tufty, 80–90cm (32–36in) | cut off faded flower stalks, then flowers until MA |
| golden spurge *Euphorbia polychroma* | yellow MSP–LSP | narrow, light green | tufty, broad, 40cm (16in) | pretty, globular growth, good autumn colouring |
| meadow iris *Iris sibirica* | violet to white, ES | grass-like | tufty, 60–80/35cm (24-32/14in) | indigenous, many beautiful varieties |
| meadow lobelia *Lobelia siphilitica* | blue, white MS–MA | light green, lancet-like | tufty, stiff, 60/40cm (24/16in) | good into autumn, absolutely hardy |
| obedient plant *Physostegia virginiana* 'Red Beauty' | lancet-like, LS–MA | denticulate | tufty, 60–80/40cm (24-32/16in) | good autumn flowerer, variety 'Vivid' even later |
| meadow rue, *Thalictrum minus* 'Adiantifolium' | yellowish ES–MS | silvery green, feathered | tufty, 50/35cm (20/14in) | graceful, with attractive leaf |
| globe flower *Trollius*-hybrids | yellow LSP–ES | hand-like, feathered | tufty, 40–60/40cm (24-32/16in) | indigenous, may flower again in autumn |
| reed *Miscanthus sinensis* | reddish EA–MA | grass-like, light coloured centre | tufty, 10–200/60cm (4-80/24in) | varieties 'Kleine Silberspinne' ('Little Silver Spider') 'Kleine Fontane' (80-120cm/32-48in) ('Little Fountain') |
| millet *Panicum virgatum* 'Strictum' | brown panicle MS–LS | green, red autumn colouring | stiff, 80–140/35cm (32-55/14) | very attractive, hardy |
| Balkan lady's mantle *Alchemilla erythropoda* | green yellow ES–MS | round, dull green | tufty, 10–20cm (4–8in) | small variety of indigenous lady's mantle |
| thrift *Armeria maritima* | red-white LSP | grass-like, shiny green | globular, 10–20cm (4–8in) | looks good all year, evergreen |
| rock cress *Arabis procurens* 'Filigree' | white LSP | small, green, red in winter | cushion–shaped, 5–15cm (2–6in) | evergreen |
| goat's beard *Aruncus aethusifolius* | cream coloured panicle, LSP–MS | large, finely feathered | bushy, 25–35cm (10–14in) | may substitute for a dwarf bush |
| bellflower *Campanula turbinata* 'Jewel' | violet, large MS–LS | small, hairy | tufty, 10–15cm (4–6in) | very attractive species |
| ivy-leaved toadflax *Cymbalaria muralis* | violet with yellow, MS–LS | small, ivy-like | creeping, 10cm (4in) | will hang over edge of trough, variety 'Compacta' is tufty |
| gentian *Gentiana sino-ornata* | radiant blue, EA–LA | small, needle-like | horizontal, 15cm (6in) | slightly acid compost, add leaf mould |
| crane's bill *Geranium subcaulescens* 'Splendens' | brilliant carmine red ES–MS | feathered | horizontal, 10cm (4in) | conspicuously strong colours |
| heath pearlwort *Sagina subulata* | small, white ES–MS | needle-like | moss-like, 2–3cm (1in) | low-growing, evergreen cushion between stones and plants |
| saxifrage *Saxifraga urbinum* 'Clarence Elliot' | pinkish red LSP–ES | round in rosettes | cushion–like, 5–8/20cm (2-3/8in) | evergreen |
| sea campion *Silene maritima* 'Weisskehlchen' | white ES–LS | small, grey green | cushion–like, 12–18cm (5–7in) | evergreen, forms lots of seed |
| grass *Festuca gautieri* 'Pic Carlit' | golden ES–LS | needle-shaped, shiny green | cushion–like, 10–25cm (4–10in) | may form large cushions, if left undisturbed, evergreen |

# Planning and preparing

## Water – the determining element of a mini pond

All water is not the same: you have to distinguish carefully between hard and soft water. A basic prerequisite for the mini pond is water that is as soft and nutrient-poor as possible.

*Hardness* Hardness is determined by the calcium and magnesium content in the water. The various degrees of hardness of water are determined as follows:

5-10 degrees Clark = soft water; 10-21 degrees Clark = medium hard water; 22-38 degrees Clark = hard water. Most plants that are suitable for mini ponds will still cope with values of hardness between 22-26 degrees Clark. You can find out the hardness value of your mains water from the local water supplier, or use a measuring device that you can obtain from the specialist trade.

*Degree of acidity* Acidity of the water is measured in pH. A value of 7 is chemically neutral. Values of 0 to 6.9 indicate acid water, and values from 7.1 to 14 mean the water is alkaline. Plants in a mini pond feel most comfortable at a pH value from 6.5 to 7, which is basically in the neutral range. The pH value should be measured from time to time, as it may alter unfavourably after certain types of weather (heavy rain fall, increased leaf fall in autumn).

*Nutrient content* Like all other plants, the plants in your mini pond will require nutrients for their wellbeing. Nutrients are dissolved in the water and absorbed by the plants' roots. The supply of nutrients should never exceed the nutrient demand of the plants, so as to maintain a biological balance in the water. This is particularly important with nitrogen in the form of nitrate compounds. Nitrates are constantly formed from organic matter together with large amounts of oxygen. If the requirement for oxygen rises sharply – possibly due to increased formation of algae in the presence of a high nitrate content in the water – too much oxygen will be removed from the water, and decomposition without oxygen will begin. This means that organic material will begin to rot.

*Measuring water values* The hardness, pH value and nitrogen content of the water can be measured with simple, inexpensive procedures. Appropriate measuring reagents, test strips and colour tables can be obtained from aquarium supply shops. This will enable every mini pond owner to determine exact water values very simply.

**My tip:** The simplest way to improve water hardness, pH values and nitrate content of pond water is by mixing the water with rainwater, which is soft, slightly acid and poor in nutrients.

## Compost

Apart from a very few plants that float in water, with or without roots, practically all others require some kind of compost into which to sink their roots. Compost can come in many different forms, depending on the requirements of the plants.

*Gravel* Gravelly material, such as that found along the course of a stream, can be bought in the specialist trade. It consists of sand and pebbles with grains of 0 to 16 or 0 to 32mm (⅝ or 1⅛in). The proportions of sand and small stones will determine how well the plants gain a hold in the bottom of the mini pond. This type of gravel does not bind with water, yet water can flow through it quite easily. Coarser gravel, without a proportion of sand, with grains of more than 30mm (1in), should only be used for covering plantations, to prevent weed growth and cut down on evaporation.

*Clay:* Clay is a good nutrient bed for water-lilies and is also suitable as a sealing material. Mud that is found in the bottom of natural ponds, for example, consists of dissolved clay and decomposed plant and animal remains. These remains are decomposed by tiny organisms and bacteria with the help of oxygen, thereby releasing nutrients that are absorbed by plants. These liberated nutrients will, as a rule, provide sufficient nutrition for your water plants.

*The choice of plants will depend on the size of the containers.*

visible shoots and display vigorous, healthy growth. When buying water-lilies, ensure that the variety name is attached. Only those varieties that appear in the table on page 14 are slow-growing and suitable for a mini pond.

Dwarf water-lilies should be in 9 to 11cm (3½ to 4¼in) deep containers. Plants that come without a firm rootball in a container must be absolutely fresh. The roots should be trimmed slightly before planting and the plant should be submerged for a little while. Surfacing plants and submerged oxygenating plants are extremely susceptible to drying out and should be transported in a sealed foil bag or in water.

**Important:** The foil bags with the plants inside should never be left in the sun. They will heat up so rapidly that the plants inside will be 'cooked' and will become unuseable. Before planting, all the plants should be laid in water for a while, or kept in a moist place.

*Composition:* The nutrients contained in the clay will not only serve as nourishment for the water plants but they will also encourage the growth of algae, so the plant compost used for a mini pond should have the kind of composition that will take account of these facts. From experience, the type of compost that is best for this purpose is relatively poor in nutrients and contains few organic components, for example, pure builders' gravel with grains of 0-16mm (⅝in). When planting water-lilies in baskets, the compost needs to be richer in nutrients because of the restricted space available, and it should consist of equal parts of clay and sand.

## Choosing and purchasing plants

The choice of and number of plants will naturally depend on the size of the container as well as your design ideas and preferences. Choose good quality when buying plants. Healthy marginal and water plants are grown in square containers with a breadth and depth of at least 9cm (3½in). The plants should have well

# Practise: planting in a mini pond

Water plants should be stored in water before planting, while you are doing the preparatory work. Submerged oxygenating plants and surfacing plants can be covered with damp newspaper or a wet cloth. Marginal and shallow water plants are more robust and will cope with a few hours without water, as long as their rootstocks are moist. The requirements of plants with respect to density and depth of water should be checked, as they can vary considerably. The employees at specialist garden centres and nurseries will be able to supply the necessary information.

## Planting in baskets
*Illustrations 1 and 2*

Plants with a rhizome (rootstock with storage capacity) are best planted inside individual lattice baskets. Planting in these baskets has the advantage that frost-sensitive water-lilies and other surfacing plants can be removed from the mini pond very easily before the winter begins. All other non-hardy plants should, therefore, be inserted into the mini pond in their own individual baskets. Planting water-lilies or other surfacing plants in baskets will only be possible if the water level is at least 15 to 20cm (6-8in) above the basket. Suitable lattice baskets are 15 to 20cm (6-8in) high, with a lattice that will allow roots to grow through.

*1 Line a basket, fill it with compost and prepare the hole for planting.*

## Unpotting

If you are intending to plant water plants in several large containers, first group the plants that are intended for each container. The chosen plants should be arranged in the container in such a way that spacing and sizes match and the appearance corresponds to your ideas. Then remove the plants from their pots. Do not tug at the tops of the plants, or the entire rootstock may break off. Turn the pot with one hand, lightly tap it on the edge of a table or similar and gently pull at the plant as it slides out. Now place the plants in position, as desired.

*2 Insert the plants, press down the compost, and add a thin layer of pebbles.*

## Planting
*Illustration 5*

When planting, pour the pure gravel or gravel mixed with clay into the spaces between the group of plants. Only put in enough gravel so that half of the rootstocks are covered. Plants that are now standing too deep in water should be placed on submerged stones, or carefully drawn up higher, allowing the gravel to slide underneath the plant. Finally, pour in more pure gravel until it reaches a level just above the rootstock. When planting water-lilies, place all the other plants into the container. Then sprinkle a little water-lily compost around the water-lilies and finally top up with gravel. Even when you plant a water-lily in its basket, you should insert all the other plants in the container first, distributing them as desired, before you fill up the container with gravel. The reverse sequence – first inserting the gravel, then the plants – is much more difficult, as the gravel continuously

*3 Fill with compost, then lay in the rhizome horizontally.*

*4 Weight the compost down a little with some pebbles.*

slides down and will squash the rootstocks flat.

## Planting water-lilies

You should take great care that the plant is not inserted too deep. The water-lily plant should be unpotted as described above, and placed with its rootstock on the base of the container. Then pour in the gravel until you can only see the tip of the shoot, which should not be covered. In order to accelerate the growth of the water-lily, insert special water-lily compost (consisting of equal parts of clay and sand) up to halfway up the rootstock, then cover with gravel.
Water-lilies that are not

in baskets will be able to spread their roots throughout the entire mini water garden and develop fully. This will only be possible with hardy varieties or in containers that are placed in a frost-free position during the winter. The other advantage is that a water-lily without a basket is not as tall and will manage with a lower plant container.

## Planting water-lilies in lattice baskets
*Illustrations 3 and 4*

A wider mesh lattice basket is more favourable for water-lilies, as this means the roots can grow out unhindered. To prevent the compost being washed out of the wider

mesh, line the basket with newspaper or hessian cloth before planting. Do not use fabric, as it will not allow roots to penetrate. Newspaper and hessian will decompose in time. Use water-lily compost for the basket and place the plant in so high that the tips of the shoots protrude 1cm (⅜in) above the edge of the basket. Then fill the basket up to 2cm (⅜in) below the inner rim with compost, press it down lightly, then cover it with gravel.

## Filling the container with water

Once your mini pond is ready and covered with gravel, fill it up with

water. We recommend placing a large sheet of paper or a flowerpot on the bottom of the container and pouring the water onto this. This will prevent the gravel being swirled about. After the container is filled with water, gently remove the paper or flowerpot again. Submerged plants should only be planted after the container has been filled with water.

*5 Fill the gaps between the plant groups with compost. Plants that end up too deep in the water should be placed on top of stones or moved to the right level.*

23

# Designing your mini ponds

A varied design in keeping with the environment will make your mini pond particularly attractive. Whether the pond is in a small basin, a wooden or stone trough or a homemade plant container, this section will provide a wealth of suggestions for attractive plant combinations and design ideas.

*Top: A floating stone and a floating candle decorate this terracotta pot with water-lilies.*
*Left: Large and small mini ponds filled with different water plants create a cheerful, colourful picture.*

# Designing your mini ponds

## The mini pond and its surroundings

Whether you decide to install your mini pond in a ceramic bowl, a wooden barrel or a large stone trough, you should ensure that the container fits harmoniously with its surroundings. A small water garden, in particular, should not be placed in isolation, but should be framed by its surroundings, in such a way that it becomes an eyecatching feature within the balcony or patio plant arrangement. You will want your little water paradise to be on view as much as possible, so you should design and arrange your mini pond in a position where you can see it, either when you look out of the window or from the balcony or patio seating area.

## Background

The mini pond will be visually emphasized if it is placed in front of a quiet, yet still appropriately designed background. Stone walls, wood-clad walls and palisades spring to mind. They can be covered with climbing plants to round off the picture. This type of background will also protect the mini pond from wind and provide a little shade.

## Neighbouring and edging plants

The mini pond should, of course, be the central feature of the plant group, and the neighbouring plants or those surrounding it should not overwhelm or disguise the water garden. Rather, they should lead the eye to the pond. On a balcony, where space is likely to be limited, large plant containers with bushes would tend to push a small water garden into the background. In the case of large, spacious patios, however, it is important to integrate the mini pond into the overall design. Here, the greater available space will allow a combination of several smaller and larger troughs. In this way, the entire area can be subdivided into easily observable sections and designed in a lively way (see also page 46).

## Climbing plants

Climbing plants can turn a balcony or patio into a green oasis provided you utilize all dimensions of the available space. Climbing plants will offer many different opportunities for design. In addition, during the summer months, they will provide higher humidity in the air due to evaporation of water, provide shade and improve the micro climate, even for the mini pond. There is a huge range of climbing plants to choose from in the garden trade. Whether you prefer brilliantly coloured flowers or calming greenery is entirely up to you. Using perennial plants, you can arrange permanent, easy-to-care-for plantations. Annual climbers will provide a flexible design. You will be able to decide anew every year what colours to choose to decorate your balcony or patio.

Another factor in the choice of plants will be whether you wish to enjoy the splendour of autumnal colours or whether you want fresh evergreen colours during the colder part of the year. Virginia creeper is attractive in the autumn with its wonderful red foliage, while ivy varieties will retain their green leaves even in the winter.

Here are a few species that will provide suitable background cover for your mini pond: evergreen honeysuckle (*Lonicera henryi*) will flourish even in a shady spot, along with the hardy clematis species (*Clematis*). Rampant amphibious bistort (*Polygonum*) and the annual climbing nasturtium (*Tropaeolum*) will cope with any position. Scented sweet peas (*Lathyrus odoratus*) will require a sunny position.

*This mini pond can be viewed from the sun lounger.*

# Designing your mini pond

### Using small basins

Small containers are, in principle, suitable for designing a mini pond and can be combined very well with larger troughs made of wood or stone. Very shallow basins or bowls with a depth of less than 10cm (4in) can, however, only be used for the creation of small marginal gardens, as the compost will barely be covered with water. In the case of tubs and basins (made of wood, clay, ceramic or plastic) with a diameter of 40 to 50cm (16 to 20in), a height of 20 to 50cm (8 to 20in) is advisable. Where deeper vessels are used, it is possible to create a complete surface of water.

### Design

A surfacing plant can be combined with a taller, upright-growing herbaceous plant and a maximum of two accompanying plants in a small plant container. This will be quite sufficient if the plants are to be effective and look good from spring through to autumn. The attractive contrast between a surfacing plant that rests flat and serenely on top of the water and a striving, upright herbaceous plant gives an interesting contrast.

### Choice of plants

A beautiful arrangement of plants will work through the contrasting shapes and colours used. Water-lilies, with their large, round leaves, will always provide a contrast to tall, slender stalks and flowers. The size of the container will determine the number of plants, and the colour of the container should, if possible, harmonize with the colours of the plants in it. Hence, delicate flower colours should be chosen for dark coloured stoneware and strongly coloured flowers should be combined with light-coloured oak.

### Planting on different levels

Square containers, from 40cm (16in) side, length and height, or round ones with a diameter of 50cm (20in) can be divided into two levels. For example, you could divide up the area for planting with a gnarled root, an interesting shaped branch or a group of attractive stones (see also pages 42–3). Stones or roots can be laid on the base of the container or can be built up from the bottom. Then, insert the plants and fill the container with gravel. This will prevent the division from shifting.

*The white water-lily goes well with the blue stoneware bowl.*

A root that is laid on the bottom layer of gravel will slide to the front when more gravel is poured in from the top up to a higher level, and will cause the remaining area of water to be diminished. The height of the level will depend on the height of the container and of the plants. If the total height of the vessel is only 20cm (8in), the lower level should be at 10cm (4in). The next level should then be at the level of the water surface.

## Planting suggestions

*Planting suggestion 1:* A dark brown stoneware tub with a diameter of 40cm (16in) and a height of 30cm (12in), is planted with the warm pink shallow water-lily 'Berthold' (*Nymphaea* 'Berthold') and the tall-growing, white striped bulrush (*Scirpus lacustris* 'Albescens').
*Planting suggestion 2:* In a light-coloured oak barrel, insert the dark red, shallow water-lily 'Froebeli' (*Nymphaea* 'Froebeli') and the slow-growing reed mace (*Typha laxmannii*).
*Planting suggestion 3:* A yellow dwarf water-lily (*Nymphaea pygmaea* 'Helvola') combined with blue pickerel weed (*Pontederia cordata)*.
If this is not enough for you, insert a third plant that only protrudes a little way above the water surface. It should only be an accompanying plant, subordinate to the other two.
*Planting suggestion 4:* A white, scented water hawthorn

(*Aponogeton distachyos*) together with a blue *Pontederia cordata* can be supplemented by a water milfoil (*Myriophyllum aquaticum*).
*Planting suggestion 5:* A red dwarf water-lily (*Nymphaea pygmaea* 'Rubra') and a crossways striped Zebra bulrush (*Scirpus* 'Zebrinus') can be combined with a white bog bean (*Menyanthes trifoliata*).
*Planting suggestion 6:* To a yellow pink water-lily (*Nymphaea* 'Chrysantha') and a variegated sweet flag (*Acorus calamus* 'Variegatus'), add a mare's tail (*Hippuris vulgaris*).
*Planting suggestion 7:* In a 20cm (8in) deep bowl, in which the upper level is at the same level as the surface of the water, insert at the edge a variegated sweet flag (*Acorus calamus* 'Variegatus') and a rush (*Juncus decipiens* 'Spiralis'), as well as, in the shallow zone (10cm/4in deep water), a water fringe plant (*Nymphoides peltata*).
*Planting suggestion 8:* In a 20cm (8in) tall container, at the edge place a marsh iris (*Iris laevigata* 'Monstrosa') and a large marsh marigold (*Caltha palustris* 'Thyermannii'); in the shallow zone (5–10cm/2–4in deep water) place a flowering rush (*Butomus umbellatus*).
*Planting suggestion 9:* Take a container that is 25cm (10in) on the inside and heighten the bank edge by a few centimetres, so that it reaches the edge of the vessel and may even protrude above it. Here, plant marsh spurge (*Euphorbia palustris*) and

a forget-me-not (*Myosotis rehsteineri*); in the shallow water (15cm/6in deep water) plant a red dwarf water-lily (*Nymphaea pygmaea* 'Rubra').
*Planting suggestion 10:* In the shallow zone (5–10cm/2–4in deep water) plant a double arrowhead (*Sagittaria latifolia* 'Plena'), a variegated sweet flag (*Acorus calamus* 'Variegatus'), and in the deep water zone (10–20cm/4–8in deep water), a white dwarf water-lily (*Nymphaea tetragona* 'Alba').

Bowls and tubs with a diameter of 30 to 50cm (12 to 20in) are particularly suitable for accommodating more vigorously growing, decorative plants that are intended to stand alone in the container. Plant these plants in the water-lily compost described on page 21, inserted into the vessel to a height of 10cm (4in) below the edge, and covered with a 2cm (⅘in) thick layer of pure gravel after the plants have been placed in the compost.
*Suitable individual plants:* common flag (*Iris pseudacorus*), sweet galingale (*Cyperus longus*), broad and narrow-leafed reed mace (*Typha latifolia* and *T. angustifolia*).

# Designing your mini pond

## Stone troughs

Troughs and planting containers made of stone can be obtained in all sizes. Due to their considerable weight, however, they can normally only be moved on rollers.

Troughs made of natural stone are particularly beautiful but very expensive, as they have to be worked from a single, large block of stone. If you are lucky, you might be able to find an old well trough or feed trough in a farmyard, that might have been removed in the course of renovating sheds or barns and has not been smashed up. Troughs made of granite or sandstone are preferable to those made of marble or limestone (containing fossil shells), as the latter will cause calcium to dissolve in the water, which some plants do not much like.

## Concrete troughs

As a rule, troughs are cast out of pure concrete without additions. They are very heavy and their surfaces can be smooth or structured, rough from the shuttering, sand-blasted or washed. As they are usually watertight, they do not need any further special treatment. By adding various other ingredients, the weight of the concrete can be lowered, but this will often render the concrete porous. If you use these lighter-weight concrete troughs for your mini water garden, you will need to coat the inside of the trough with a waterseal paint. Obtain a sealant from the building trade and apply two coats.

**My tip:** To make your own sealing compound, use half a litre (1 pint) of skimmed milk and mix in enough cement to create a thick, liquid mass that can be painted on.

## Concrete rings

The large rings that are used for drainage, and similar projects, come with diameters of 80/100/120/150cm (32/40/48/60in) and in heights of 25 or 30cm (10 or 12in). These rings can be assembled in groups of various sizes and heights on larger roof gardens and will look rather attractive. As they are open at the bottom, they will need to be closed.

For this task, place the ring on a layer of something like newspaper, or plastic liner that will prevent the bottom edge of the ring from being in contact with the ground. Then, pour in the concrete for the floor of the container. The concrete should be moist but not wet, should be stamped down well, and then rubbed in with a short length of plank, until the top surface is wet. To be absolutely safe, finally paint the floor and inside walls of the container with a sealing agent.

## Design

With their generally longish shape, stone and concrete troughs present more possibilities than round containers, as different depths of water can be created in one vessel. To obtain a particularly attractive effect, lift part of the planting area above the water surface. This will enable you to create a typical pond bank situation on one side and a corresponding water surface on the other. Plants for marginal, shallow water and deep water zones can all be accommodated in such an arrangement. The different heights are best built with graduated levels of gravel. As gravel 'loses' half its weight in water, it does not lie very firmly and easily slides to the bottom. So, the difference in levels should not exceed 30 percent or the compost/material used for planting will simply slide to the bottom as soon as the trough is filled with water.

## Planting suggestions

If the trough is designed purely as a deep water zone, you will only need to choose between water-lilies and shallow water plants that can cope with a depth of 25cm (10in) or more.

*Troughs made of natural stone are worked from a single block of stone.*

**Planting suggestion 1:** For the deep water zone (20–30cm/ 8–12in), plant a red shallow water-lily (*Nymphaea laydekeri* 'Purpurata'), a grey brown reed mace (*Typha shuttleworthii*), and a striped sweet grass (*Glyceria maxima* 'Variegata'); for the submerged plant, choose a rigid hornwort (*Ceratophyllum demersum*).
**Planting suggestion 2:** In the deep water zone (20–30cm/ 8–12in), plant a white dwarf water-lily (*Nymphaea tetragona* 'Alba'), arrowhead (*Sagittaria sagittifolia*) and striped rush (*Scirpus lacustris* 'Albescens'); add submerged plant water

crowfoot (*Ranunculus aquatilis*).
Two planting levels enable you to choose from a larger selection of plants. The second level can be created as a shallow water zone or a marginal zone.
**Planting suggestion 3:** In the shallow water zone (15cm/6in deep water) plant striped rush (*Scirpus lacustris* 'Albescens'), water plantain (*Alisma plantago-aquatica*), reed mace (*Typha laxmannii*), Japanese iris (*Iris laevigata*) and bog bean (*Menyanthes trifoliata*); in the deep water zone (30cm/12in) try the pink shallow water-lily (*Nymphaea* 'Berthold'); and for the submerged plant, try the

rush (*Eleocharis acicularis*).
**Planting suggestion 4:** In the marginal zone (0 to 2cm/0 to 1in), plant a grey brown reed mace (*Typha shuttleworthii*), a bog bean (*Menyanthes trifoliata*), a yellow creeping-Jenny (*Lysimachia nummularia* 'Aurea'), a spiral rush (*Juncus effesus* 'Spiralis'), and a bog arum (*Calla palustris*); for the deep water zone (20cm/8in deep water), choose striped rush (*Scirpus lacustris* 'Albescens'), and a pink water-lily (*Nymphaea carolinia* 'Perfecta').
You will be able to choose from the entire selection of water plants for an installation that has three planting levels.
**Planting suggestion 5:** In the marginal zone (0 to 5cm/0 to 2in), pick a yellow hosta (*Hosta* 'Golden Tiara'), a red candelabra primrose (*Primula japonica* 'Miller's Crimson'), and a loosestrife (*Lythrum virgatum* 'Rose Queen'); in the shallow water zone (5–10cm/2–4in), plant marsh pennywort (*Hydrocotyle novae-zelandiae*), white marsh forget-me-not (*Myosotis palustris* 'Alba'), a water plantain with heart-shaped leaves (*Alisma subcordata*), mare's tail (*Hippuris vulgaris*),a sweet flag (*Acorus calamus* 'Variegatus') and a rush (*Eleocharis acicularis*); for the deep water zone (20–30cm/ 8–12in deep water) choose a pink water-lily (*Nymphaea laydekeri* 'Lilacea').

# Designing your mini pond

## Barrels of fun with water

The planting suggestions in the section on 'stone and concrete troughs' can also be applied to the larger wooden containers. These troughs can be purchased in garden centres, builders' merchants or DIY stores in a great variety of sizes and shapes (square, rectangular or hexagonal). The smallest are not much larger than a regular flower box, while the largest may be up to 120cm (48in) long, 80cm (32in) wide, and 30 to 50cm (12–20in) tall. Planting containers made of wood can be obtained as ready-made troughs or in kit form. Still extremely popular are halved whiskey barrels (now a rarity due to demand), halved herring and beer barrels, as well as old wooden wash tubs.

## Troughs with inserts

The ready-made wooden troughs for sale in the trade are intended for use as flower boxes, so they are not watertight. You should be able to obtain appropriate inserts for troughs, that can be hung inside smaller troughs and stood inside larger ones. Equipped in this way, different-sized wooden planting containers can be turned into attractive mini ponds. You should be able to obtain inserts for hexagonal boxes with a diameter of 70cm (28in), for square boxes with a side length of 40, 50 and 60cm (16,20 and 24in), as well as for rectangular wooden troughs with the following dimensions: 40 x 60cm, 40 x 80cm, 40 x 100cm and 40 x 120cm (16 x 24, 32, 40 and 48in). The inside measurements of wooden tubs are correspondingly smaller, and approximately 10cm (4in) should be subtracted from the length and width.

## Troughs without inserts

These troughs need to be clad on the inside with a watertight liner. If you plan to transport or move them about later on, it would be preferable to provide them with a floor, so the liner is not damaged from below when moving the trough. Wooden frames without a floor will only be suitable if the resting place for the mini pond is definitely final. Once the liner is resting on the ground beneath, the trough may no longer be moved about, or slid around, and will need to be cleared out for even a minor move. Place a layer of fabric under the frame to protect the liner. Once the liner has been fitted to the trough, and the trough is filled with water, gravel and plants, the fabric that protrudes under the trough can be cut off all round with a sharp knife. This provides good protection from below for the liner, and also a flexible base that will give better under the pressure from above.

## Planting suggestions:
*(for troughs with three levels)*

*Planting suggestion 1:* In the marginal zone (0–5cm/0–2in deep water): a large marsh marigold (*Caltha palustris* 'Thyermannii'), a rockery primrose (*Primula rosea*), an iris (*Iris setosa*), a loosestrife (*Lythrum virgatum* 'Dropmore Purple'); in the shallow water zone (5–10cm/2–4in deep water): a water plantain with narrow leaves (*Alisma lanceolata*), bog bean (*Menyanthes trifoliata*), a flowering rush (*Butomus umbellatus* 'Rose Red'), a zebra rush (*Scirpus tabernaemontani* 'Zebrinus'); and in the deep water zone (20–30cm/8–12in deep water): a dwarf water-lily (*Nymphaea pygmaea* 'Graziella'), rigid hornwort (*Ceratophyllum demersum*).

*Planting suggestion 2:* In the marginal zone (0–5cm/0–2in deep water): a bugle (*Ajuga reptans* 'Atropurpurea'), a spurge (*Euphorbia palustris*), a giant yellow cowslip (*Primula florindae*), a marsh fern (*Thelipteris palustris*); in the shallow zone (5–10cm/2–4in deep water): an iris (*Iris laevigata* 'Dorothea'), golden club (*Orontium aquaticum*), an arrowhead (*Sagittaria latifolia* 'Plena'), a grey brown reed mace (*Typha shuttleworthii*); and in the deep zone (20–30cm/ 8–12in deep water): a water soldier (*Stratiotes aloides*), and a water fringe (*Nymphoides peltata*).

*Half-barrels made of wood are popular plant containers for mini water gardens.*

# Practise: sealing wooden troughs

Remember that wooden troughs used as planting containers for mini ponds require a liner to make them watertight.

## Liners

You should always use a good quality 'pond liner' for your mini pond. Cheaper products are often of inferior quality, are more susceptible to tearing, do not stretch well, and can contain harmful substances. We recommend a UV-stabilized pond liner that is harmless for water plants. Although stabilizing the liner against UV rays is not strictly necessary for a mini water garden, it is nevertheless a quality feature of a good PVC pond liner.

PVC liners, however, have been causing much controversy in recent years, because their manufacture and use is strongly environmentally unfriendly. In addition, getting rid of them after use is creating ever more problems. Butyl liners are an environmentally friendly alternative. Butyl rubber is an organic latex compound and liners made of this material can be thermically disposed of, without creating harmful gases or waste matter. These liners are easy to work with as, in contrast with PVC, they remain flexible even at low temperatures. A further advantage is the long-term stability of accurate measurements. PVC liners tend to shrink if they are not fixed to an entire surface. Butyl liners also last longer and are more durable under UV rays. The drawback is that they are generally much more expensive than PVC liners.

## Liner thickness

PVC liners and butyl liners can be obtained in various different thicknesses from 0.5 to 2 mm. Although 0.5 mm should be sufficient for a mini pond, we recommend a liner with a thickness of 0.8 to 1 mm, to provide protection against damage and to ensure it seals well.

## Measuring the liner
*Illustration 1*

First establish the inside measurements of the trough you wish to use for your mini pond, and measure them out on the liner. To be on the safe side, add another 2 to 5cm (¾ to 2in) all round, so you can later allow for minor adjustments. It is very annoying to find you are short of a centimetre or two at the end.

## Inserting and attaching the liner
*Illustrations 2 and 3*

Start with one of the two long sides, when you lay the liner into the trough. Mark, both on the trough and the liner, the exact centre point of the side, make sure these points are exactly lined up, then staple the liner along this edge to the corners (illustration 2). After this, the liner should be folded at the two corners of the trough and tacked into position. Press the liner firmly into the corners. You will now discover that the liner can only

*1 Transfer the inner measurements of the trough onto the liner, adding 2 to 5cm (¾ to 2in) all round, to be safe, so that slippage is catered for.*

4 Fix the liner to the sides with an aluminium retaining strip, then cut off the excess liner.

## Cutting the liner
*Illustration 4*

Before cutting the liner, make sure that it fits snugly in the corners and along the edges, and that all undesirable wrinkles have been smoothed out. The best way to check this is by filling the trough with water. Then staple the liner to the edges of the trough – for example, with a narrow aluminium retaining strip that can be screwed to the liner. Only at this point should the excess liner be trimmed off. Another idea is to screw a wooden or plastic angle piece to the insides of the trough, but the liner should be cut off before doing this. If you are using a PVC liner, it will be necessary to staple it along the entire length of the trough, because it might shrink, as mentioned above. A butyl liner merely needs to be attached at a few key points with a screw and a collar.

be folded properly if it has been fixed at the right height for that side. To prevent the liner stretching later on, it must be pressed properly into all the corners and edges. There should be no wrinkles from stretching, either on the trough walls or on the floor of the trough. Provided you do not staple the liner on with no extra margin left, but allow a centimetre overlap, you can later smooth it down and re-staple it, if necessary.
**My tip:** Ensure that the liner fits snugly into the corners and remains there, by taking a shovelful of sand and pressing it tightly into the corner (see illustration 3).
You will now be able to staple the fold obtained along the long side of the trough. The fold in

the liner, that runs diagonally to the corner, will be clearly visible. It looks even better if the fold lies behind the liner, so that the latter remains basically smooth and tidy, and the groove is exactly vertical in the corner. If you have worked neatly, the edge of the liner should be visible everwhere along the top of the trough. The fold or groove in the corner should not seem to disappear towards the floor of the trough.

2 Mark the centre of the liner and the trough edge and staple.

3 Press the liner down firmly at the corners with a shovelful of sand.

# Designing your mini pond

## Compost for the outer trough

Composts containing peat or bark are unsuitable for a permanent planting. Both substances decompose quickly, leading to subsidence. Even after a short time, the inner trough will protrude above the surrounding planting. The alternative is a mineral compost that retains its structure, for example, gravel, sand or clay. These substances are, unfortunately, rather heavy, and cannot be used in large quantities on balconies or roof gardens. They can, however, be substituted with lighter materials, for example, special 'roof garden compost'.

**My tip:** You can make the compost for the inner trough yourself, if you follow this recipe: 4 buckets of broken aggregate, 2 buckets bark compost, 2 buckets clay or loamy garden soil and 100g (3½oz) organic-mineral mixed fertilizer.

## Overflow

Occasionally, after a heavy downpour of rain or if you have overwatered, the water level in the inner trough may rise to the edge, so that the plants surrounding the mini pond are practically standing in water. To prevent this happening, bore a hole through the liner above the layer of aggregate, and through the outer wall of the trough. Pick a side that is not visible. The excess water can then flow away to the outside.

To prevent water running down the outer wall of the trough, we recommend installing a drainage device through the wall, that will ensure the trough remains dry. Use a 1cm (⅜in) thick brass pipe for the purpose, with its thread on the outside, that can be turned through the hole you have

## Tub within a tub – the mini water landscape

By placing together several smaller containers inside a larger trough or tub, and planting around them, you can create a regular small landscape.

A wooden trough or framework (outer trough or outer tub), that is at least 60cm (24in) wide inside, 100cm (40in) long and 50cm (20in) deep, is lined with a pond liner and filled with aggregate by about 8 to 10cm (3 to 4in).

Stand the tub (innertub) or the basin for the mini pond on top of this. The aggregate serves as a water reservoir for the plants around the mini ponds. In the spaces between the aggregate pellets, water can collect, rise up and supply the plants above with moisture. To prevent the spaces between the aggregate filling up with compost or soil, rather than water, cover the aggregate with a piece of fabric.

bored and fixed with two screws and a collar. A plastic household sponge or similar can be used to protect the overflow pipe from becoming clogged with aggregate granules. Only then lay in the fabric.

## Inserting an inner trough or tub

Now you can place the planting container for the mini pond inside the wooden trough or tub. The upper edge of the vessel should lie a little below the edge of the outer trough. In our example, a small mortar mixing bowl, made of plastic, 40cm (16in) wide, 60cm (24in) long, and up to 40cm (16in) deep, makes a good small vessel for the purpose. It can remain filled with water in winter, without bursting in frosty weather. Before placing the compost in it, plant water plants in the small vessel and fill it up with water (see Practise: planting, pages 22-3).

## Plants for the outer trough or tub

In principle, all herbaceous plants that do not grow too large can be used for planting around the mini pond. Plants that grow in water meadows will work best in a mini water garden. The background can be created with a few beautiful, not too tall grasses, in front of which herbaceous plants half that size are grouped, and they gradually

become shorter the closer they get to the front of the arrangement. Between them and round the edge of the inner tub, plant a few creeping, ground-covering species that will cover the edge of the trough or tub, or even hang over it.

The plants in the tables on pages 14–15 and 18–19 will offer plenty of scope for making your own designs.

## Suggestion for planting

The following planting suggestion is intended to stimulate your own creativity, or you can go back and choose or adapt the planting suggestions made in previous sections.

The outer trough is 120cm (48in) long and 60cm (24in) wide. The inner tub measures 35 x 60cm (14 x 24in) and is placed in the front right-hand corner. This means you obtain an area, to the left of the inner tub, that is about 60 x 60cm (24 x 24in), and behind it, an area of about 25 x 60cm (10 x 24in).

Place only two plants in the inner tub: a pink water-lily (*Nymphaea* 'Berthold') and a reed mace (*Typha laxmannii*). In the outer trough, plant a fan maple (*Acer palmatum* 'Dissectum Atropupureum') and behind the inner tub, approximately in the centre, a yellow-leafed spindle berry (*Euonymus fortunei* 'Emerald 'n' Gold'). A variegated hosta (*Hosta siboldii*) should be arranged so that its leaves dangle over the

back corner of the inner tub.

Over the remaining free area, distribute one each of the following: a dwarf bellflower (*Campanula turbinata* 'Jewel'), a drumstick primrose (*Primula denticula*), an autumn gentian (*Gentiana sino-ornata*), a creeping-Jenny (*Lysimachia nummularia*), a candelabra primrose (*Primula japonica* 'Miller's Crimson'), a thrift (*Armeria maritima*), a sea campion (*Silene maritima*) and a lady's Mantle (*Alchemilla erythropoda*).

All of these plants are hardy and can be overwintered in the trough.

**Important:** When planting in your miniature water landscape, make absolutely sure that you place the plants that grow tall in the outer trough, right at the back, and plant the low-growing ones at the front. Tall plants in the foreground would hinder your view of the mini pond and the other plants.

# Designing your mini pond

## Building your own mini pond

Naturally you can, if you wish, build your own small or large plant containers for your mini pond. Decide, first, if you want to be able to move them about once there are plants in them, or whether they are intended to stand in the same position permanently. A trough containing plants will be transportable, if its weight allows, if it has a firm floor, or if the watertight cladding on the inside consists of a rigid tub or similar.

## Framing a mortar mixing bowl

Mortar mixing bowls can be surrounded quite simply with a framework made of wood, of the same height, that is placed over the bowl. The frame and the bowl will then rest on the floor/ground and can be moved separately at any time. A more permanent fixture is achieved if the bowl is hung into the framework. Screw a batten to the inside of the frame that runs 2 to 3 mm higher than the bottom edge of the upper edge of the bowl. This will make the frame more stable, and the bowl will hang by the upper edge, while the bottom of the bowl that is under pressure, due to the load of compost, plants and water, will rest on the ground. This measure will also prevent the bowl from bulging outward

once it contains plants and water, which might otherwise press against the frame and make it give way.

## Troughs built of brick or stone

All kinds of materials from clinker bricks to tiles to natural stone can be used for building your own trough. Before starting work, to be on the safe side, lay a piece of fabric or a piece of pond liner on the ground, in order to avoid damaging the balcony floor or patio tiles, or making them excessively dirty. This will also mean that later on, if the trough has to be dismantled again, the balcony or patio can be restored to their original state. Usually, when laying bricks or similar for a trough, the surrounding area will also tend to get dirty, so the piece of liner should be larger. When the work is finished, cut off the protruding sections of liner right back to the edge of the trough.
   Use cement mortar for building the trough, in a mixing ratio of 4 to 5 parts sand to one part cement. The wall of the trough should definitely be at least as wide as the width of a brick, to ensure it is stable. The inside should be rendered. The walls should be slightly sloping, if you intend to leave water in the trough during the winter. Before laying the top layer of bricks, place the liner in the trough, and

arrange it over half of the top edge of bricks, then cement the top layer of bricks on top of the liner.

## Securing the trough against frost

Water expands when it freezes, and this expansion may release considerable force. The pressure builds from the top to the bottom, as water freezes first on the surface. The deeper the water freezes, the greater the pressure on the bottom, and also sideways. To prevent mini pond troughs that are left to overwinter outside from bursting in frosty weather, they can either be emptied, or built in such a way that they withstand the pressure of ice.

## Sloping walls

Sloping walls enable freezing water to be diverted upwards. A flatter angle is more favourable than a steep one, so a slope of 15 percent is recommended. In a 50cm (20in) tall wooden trough, for example, the upper edges of the sides should be 7 to 8cm (3in) longer per side than at the floor of the trough.

*The mini pond can be framed with a palisade fence.*

As a rule, building one long side with the two short sides sloping outwards will be sufficient. In the case of very open and frost-endangered troughs, it might be better to slope all four sides. The incorporation of sloping sides into ready-made or home-built troughs should be carried out before sealing the container with a liner.

## Building in sloping sides

A good material to use is the pressure-resistant, expanding foam sheet that builders use for insulating walls, ceilings and floors. These sheets can be obtained with the dimensions 50 x 100cm (20 x 40in) and with a thickness of 1-16cm (⅜-6in). The thickness of sheets required will depend on the height of the trough walls. A sheet about 8cm (3in) thick, will be sufficient for a trough with a height of 50cm (20in). The foam sheet should be cut diagonally and lengthwise in order to obtain two equally shaped wedges (at 1m/40in long, they will be 7.5cm/3in at the top and 0.5cm/⅛in wide at the bottom). If the foam sheets are wider, wedges should be built in on all sides. If you decide to insert a wedge on three sides only, the wedge on the long side should be turned towards the sun, if at all possible. On sunny, clear, frosty days the sun will shine through the ice and warm up the foam sheet enough to melt the ice to a thin film of water between the ice and the liner. The ice can move up and down this thin film of water and equalize the pressure. The insulating effect of the wedge underneath also encourages a warming up of the liner.

## Wedges for stone or concrete troughs

Protecting stone and concrete troughs against frost is accomplished in a similar fashion to that described for wooden troughs above. The wedges, made of aerated concrete, for example, are cut to size, inserted with mortar and then rendered. Line the trough with a pond liner.

39

# Practise: building your own wooden troughs

The size and shape of a mini pond can be matched exactly to your specifications when you build your own wooden trough. Wood is a material that is easy to work and is a particularly good alternative to a ready-made trough for someone who wants to engage in some DIY without a great deal of fuss and effort. When planning your trough, do give some consideration to overwintering it: for example, do you want to build in sloping walls to protect it against frost (see pages 38-9)? You may use nails or screws for fixing the wooden parts together, or even use cross-head screws.

## A trough made of planks

First, select the wood. Choose among planks of different thicknesses and widths. For troughs of about 1m (40in) length, planks 16–18cm (6–7in) thick will suffice. For longer troughs, the planks should be 22–24mm (⅞in) thick. The plank should be carefully measured and cut; the saw cut should

*1 To join the short and long ends together, fix pieces of batten inside the right and left of the short ends and screw together.*

run at a 90° angle to the edge of the plank and be very straight. The greater the need for exact measurements, the more useful it is to make a sketch or drawing first. Determine whether the long edges or the short edges should be enclosed, which means either placing the long planks between the short end ones or the short end planks between the long ones. Where the first option is concerned, the screws used for fixing should be situated on the short sides of the trough; in the second option, the screws will be on the long sides of the

trough. Whichever option you choose, it will make hardly any difference for small containers. In the case of long troughs, it is recommended to enclose the short side planks.

## Calculating the material

If, for example, you want to build a wooden trough that is 80cm (32in) long and 40cm (16in) wide (on the outside), that will be enclosed at the short ends, the plank used for the short ends will have to be shortened, on both ends, by the thickness of the planks used. For 16mm (⅞in) thick planks, the short ends of the trough will measure 36.8cm (14½in). A trough without a floor, with a height of 40cm (16in), will require four planks that are 80cm (32in) long and 20cm (8in) wide, as well as four planks that are 36.8cm (14½in) long and 20cm (8in) wide.

## Putting it all together
*Illustrations 1 and 2*

All would be so easy if the screws were to fit into the short side planks without any ado. This will, however, only be the case, if they are screwed into the wood at a right angle to the direction of wood growth. In order to fix the short end planks to the long side ones, you will need to place a batten or narrow plank, on the inside, on both sides of the short end planks, and screw the long planks to the batten (illustration 1).

In the case of larger troughs with longer side walls, you should connect the planks of one long side to each other, by means of a small batten on the inside, that is secured at intervals of 50 to 60cm (20 to 24in). This will prevent the long planks from slipping or sliding against each other.

Either fix the floor securely to the trough, or lay it in loose. For the fixed version, screw a batten to the inside of the long planks at the bottom, then lay the flooring planks in and fix them (see illustration 2). For a removable floor, proceed in the same way, but do not fix the planks to the trough itself, but to two battens lying on the ground, to stop the floor planks from slipping. The corners of the floor will need portions cut out of them to fit around the vertical battens in the corners.

## A trough made of ready sawn timber
*Illustration 3*

Sawn timber, measuring 6 x 8cm, 8 x 10cm or 8 x 12cm (2 x 3in, 3 x 4in or 4 x 5in) is ideal for building a trough. The timber will be very strong but difficult to transport. A trough made of sawn timber should, therefore, only be placed somewhere it can remain permanently. Cutting the wood will depend on whether the pieces are used lying on their wider or narrower edges. You will save time and money if you build them together by placing them, one above the other, on

*2 Fix a batten in to take the floor of the trough.*

*3 Drill two holes at one end and one hole at the other end and join the timbers firmly together with wooden dowels.*

their narrower edge (see illustration 3). When calculating the lengths of the individual sides, subtract the thickness of the 'narrower' thickness only once from each length. This will enable you to stagger the corners of the trough. Alternate, or stagger the way the long and short lengths of wood meet at the corner (see illustration 3); this creates greater stability and will prevent the individual pieces from being pushed out. To fix the pieces of wood particularly securely, drill three holes – two at one end, one at the other – and connect the holes with wooden dowels (see illustration 3). For 6 mm thick dowels, drill holes that are only 5.5 mm across.

When creating a half-overlap joint, all the lengths of timber are cut either to the length or breadth of the trough. At both ends of each piece, take out a piece that is half of the height and the whole width of the timber. This will enable you to overlap at the corners and you will need only one joining point.

# Designing your mini pond

## Connecting a power source

The installation of lighting and fountains in a mini pond requires a special, secured connection to a mains electricity supply on the balcony or patio.

There are legal regulations concerning the installation of a 240 volt alternating current from the mains system for outside use, particularly when water is involved. Should you desire to install a pump or a light in your mini pond, you will need to check that your fuse box has a special circuit breaker. This device will turn off the supply, even if the current differs by an imperceptible 30 milliamperes. If you do not possess a residual circuit breaker, buy one in an electrical supply shop and insert it between the outlet and the outside installation. Better still is to use a low voltage transformer (12 or 24 volt).

**Important:** There are a great variety of ways to connect a power source to the outside, so obtain advice from an expert, preferably at the place where you buy lights or pumps for your mini pond.

## Lighting

Low voltage spotlights, that can be employed both under water and above, are one idea for your mini pond. These lights use a bundled beam and are mainly appropriate for lighting up an individual plant or fountain. The output of these spots ranges from 20 watt upwards, but the light can appear rather hard and bright. These lights are less suitable underwater, as they tend to warm up the water. For this purpose, preferably choose an underwater light of 5 watts, which will attractively illuminate the entire area of water from below.

**My tip:** Place the light as close as possible to the inside of the front wall of your mini pond container. This will prevent it from creating an irritating glare when you step close to the trough. Conduct the electrical cable through the gravel and behind a plant, over the top edge of the trough, to the back. Should you wish to illuminate a bubbling stream of water, stand the light directly behind the pump or fix it to the upward pipe of the bubbler.

The specialist trade offers a selection of attractively designed and variably useable 12 watt spots with small 10 watt halogen lamps for outside lighting.

## Decoration

Your mini pond will be especially charming if you include a beautiful stone here or there, a gnarled root or even a small sculpture. This will also give a more relaxed look to your grouping of plants. Stones and roots not only cover up edges, ugly corners and technical equipment, but they will also prevent the gravel in the different levels from sliding to the bottom. In addition, stones can be used to create a third planting level – the moist zone – if they are arranged above the surface of the water, and gravel is shored up behind them.

## Stones and roots

Stones and roots of different sizes and shapes can be employed in a mini pond. Stones are an important building element in larger containers, that can be used to create different depths of water or a raised bank area. Suitable stones are stocked by builders' merchants, natural stone suppliers, landscape gardeners, zoological suppliers and garden centres. Basalt tuff is particularly recommended as it is relatively light in weight and free of calcium, but it is not cheap. In principle, use any stone that can have a hole drilled through it to make a bubbler. Erratic stones with conspicuous shapes or even worked stone made of granite, as well as old millstones, are suitable for the purpose. Bubble stones can also be bought ready-made in the trade. Roots that are to be used in your mini water garden should not be fresh, but should have been dead for several years and look weathered. Roots of bog trees are recommended, as they can be used above or below water.

*Floating stones and small sculptures provide decorative features in a miniature water garden.*

Old oak roots or gnarled oak branches, when they have lain in water for a few days, will become so heavy that they will no longer float to the top.

## Sculptures

Attractive accents can be created in your miniature water landscape with small sculptures and water ornaments. They will form pretty, eyecatching features inside the water basin or in the design of the balcony or patio as a whole. There is a huge range of items to choose from.

# Practise: fountains and water reservoirs

Moving water, whether flowing, gently splashing or rising in a small fountain, has a charm of its own. It has a calming effect on the ear and eye of the observer and helps to heighten the magnetic allure of the mini water garden.

**Important:** Water-lilies and fountains do not go together and should be kept in separate containers. The splashing of water means the water-lilies' leaves are constantly wet on top, can no longer breathe properly and will begin to decay.

## Pumps
*Illustrations 1 and 2*

It is easy to get moving water by installing a pump (see connecting to a power source, page 42). The size and type of plants in your mini pond will determine the choice of pump. Seek advice

from an expert in your local garden centre or somewhere similar. Stand the pump on the bottom of the deep water zone of the trough and cover it with a few larger stones. Now you need to determine the desired height and force of the bubbling stream of water. Fix a PVC pipe to the pump, allow it to end just under the surface of the water, and switch on the pump. If the stream of water is too high, shorten the pipe until the stream has the height and force you want. Basically, the following rule applies: if the top of the pipe is just below the surface, water will be ejected upwards in a steep, narrow fountain (illustration 1); the

lower the end of the pipe is below the surface, the broader the stream of water (see illustration 2).

## Bubble stones and filters
*Illustration 3*

Bubble stones that have water running over them not only look very attractive in a mini pond, but can also be used to filter the water. You will need a plastic pipe with a diameter of 10cm (4in), that ends about 3cm (1⅛in) beneath the bank zone. Saw a number of small slits into the pipe, or drill holes in it to make it sieve-like, so the pump is able to suck up water from the surrounding gravel. This turns the gravel into a

filter. Attach the bottom of the pipe to a pump with an output of 5 to 6 litres (9 to 10 pints) per minute. Cover the top end of the pipe with a stone that is connected to the pump by a length of hose.

## Installing a water reservoir

As long as you check the water level once or twice a week, that should be sufficient to control water loss in a mini pond. Replenish water lost by evaporation with a watering can. Troughs with a raised bank zone will suffer from a much higher rate of evaporation than troughs with a overall surface of water. The buildup of stones and gravel in a bank zone will often reduce the amount of water in the trough by a third or a quarter.
If you find the water level in the trough sinks very rapidly, this is because the small volume of water present has to make up for loss of water through evaporation from the entire trough. Employing an additional

*1 A bubbling jet rises steeply.*

*2 The bubbling jet is flat and wide.*

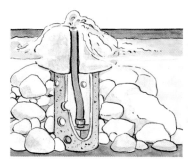

*3 A bubble stone should be placed in such a way that the water can flow back into the pond.*

water reservoir will ensure that water loss is slowed down.

## A storage device
*Illustration 4*

Before filling the trough with gravel, make a hollow space in the area of the bank zone, at the bottom of the trough, that can be filled with water. An upside-down flowerpot is ideal for the purpose and should be placed on the bottom of the trough. A few notches cut out of the top edge of the pot, or placing the pot on a thin layer of gravel, will ensure that water can enter the pot from below.

## And this is how the water reservoir works
*Illustration 4*

The water penetrating the flowerpot will displace air from it, that can escape through the hole. Make sure the hole is never clogged up by placing a shard on it. After placing the pot in the trough, fill the trough with Hortag, so that even the shard on top of the pot is covered. Air will be able to escape from the pot and can penetrate it again when the water level drops.

Then pour gravel onto the water reservoir and plant your water plants on top. The gravel layer needs to be at least 10cm (4in) thick, so the top of the water reservoir should end about 10 to 12cm (4 to 5in) below the edge of the trough. Then, when you fill the trough with water, the water will penetrate the hollow space inside the flowerpot from below, while air can escape through the hole in the top of the flowerpot. If the hole becomes clogged up, the flowerpot will float to the top and the whole planting arrangement will be destroyed. The stored volume of water enables the water in the free part of the trough to be replenished, so that the level of water in the entire container will sink at a lower rate.

*4 Surround the water reservoir with aggregate, place compost on top, and insert the plant.*

# Designing your mini pond

## A little oasis on your balcony – mini pond variations

A seating area by a pond and a place for quiet contemplation – this is something most garden owners dream of. Even on a balcony or patio, building a small water garden oasis will invite you to linger and relax.

An area of at least 6 sq m (7 sq yards) was used for the following design ideas. The planting suggestions have been kept fairly general, to leave enough scope for personal ideas when ordering and arranging plants.

### A breath of the Far East

Diagonally to the front left corner of the balcony, arrange the planting combination in larger and smaller ceramic containers, the centre of which is taken up by the mini pond.

Plant a pink shallow-water water-lily and a variegated rush in a low, wide bowl. The Far Eastern impression is provided by a Japanese fountain (*Shishi-Odoshi*) made of bamboo (obtainable from most garden centres), which works on an astonishingly simple mechanical principle and is particularly fascinating. A bamboo plant should provide the background for the mini pond. An azalea-hybrid, a fan maple, and a rhododendron bush form a framework on either side. Group various small pots with variegated hostas and lady's mantle between the large plant containers. Then you might decide to place a bamboo espalier with a clematis and a seating group made of a dark-coloured rattan opposite the entire planting group.

## A water landscape with a palisade fence

Again, running diagonal to one corner of the balcony, place a palisade fence in a gentle curve, which provides the front setting for a mini water landscape (see photo, page 39). Behind the fence, arrange two mini ponds in rectangular planters with a surrounding planting of various different herbaceous plants and ornamental bushes.

One trough should contain reed mace, arrowhead and a hornwort. An appropriate pump will create a small fountain rising up from among the plants.

In the second trough, a water-lily with a dark-coloured flower, a marsh marigold, a flowering rush, as well as a mare's tail, will ensure an attractive, brilliant play of colour.

At the other side of the balcony, three oleander bushes in light-coloured wooden troughs will create a fairly open visual screen of filigree leaves and blooms. Then, a seating arrangement made of light-coloured wood may be placed in the centre of the balcony.

## A patio with natural stone troughs

The greater space available on a patio will allow a more generous and elaborate arrangement of plants. Nevertheless, the weight-bearing capacity of the patio should be checked beforehand. In the front righthand corner of the patio, place three natural stone troughs, troughs 1 and 2 vertically to each other, trough 3 parallel and slightly displaced towards the front of trough 2. Trough 1 can be designed as a marginal bed with various different marginal plants. Trough 2 will contain the mini pond with water-lilies or other surfacing plants. Trough 3 is filled with rockery herbaceous plants. The visual screen for a cast iron seating group in front of the right-hand wall of the house is formed by a pergola at right angles, covered in various flowering climbing plants. Several evergreen container plants placed in a half round delimit the seating group on the opposite side of the patio, thereby creating a more intimate atmosphere.

*A pleasant, contemplative seating area can be created on a balcony.*

# Care and overwintering

Once you have succeeded in designing and creating a mini pond, ensure the continuing success of your creation with regular, methodical maintenance, to keep the arrangement looking attractive and the water fresh and clean. Suggestions and tips for successful overwintering will round off the programme of care for your mini pond.

*Top: The carmine red flowers of the shallow-water water-lily Nymphaea laydekeri 'Purpurata' are slightly lighter around the outside edges.*
*Left: Exotic water and marginal plants, like lotus flowers and very stiff rush types, are sensitive to frost and will have to be overwintered in a frost-free, bright room.*

# Care and overwintering

## Clean and healthy water

After the water has been standing in a trough for a while, a biological equilibrium should establish itself in your mini pond. The mud at the bottom should be home to exactly the right kind of micro-organisms that will ensure the decomposition of organic matter, thereby playing a part in keeping the water clear. You need to pay special attention to the water to ensure that this biological equilibrium is maintained. The most important measure of care has to be regular topping up, as the water level should never be allowed to fluctuate too much. In warm weather, check the water every other day, if possible, and top up if necessary.

## The pH value

Depending on the quality of your mains supply, use water straight from the tap, or make sure the pH is favourable (between 6 and 6.5) by adding rainwater. Check the pH value every 4 to 6 weeks, using a test strip you can obtain from an aquarium supply shop. Any changes in the colour of the test strip should be checked against the accompanying colour scale, where you can read off the degree of acidity or alkalinity. Other ways of testing include filling a small transparent container with pondwater, colouring the water with an indicator solution, and then comparing it against a scale. If the water is too acidic (pH 5.5 or less), insert a few limestones or a little marble gravel in the water. The carbon dioxide in the water will dissolve a little calcium from these stones and the pH should rise. If the pH is too high, adding rainwater will be the best solution. Should the value still remain higher than 7.5, you should check the gravel or the stones in your mini pond. You might need to replace plants that do not like an alkaline medium with others that can stand lime in the water.

## Getting rid of algae

The dreaded filamentous algae, that creates a cottonwool-like, green web of fine, thin fibres, thrives in water with a high pH containing lime. A pH value of 6 will ensure that this organism does not become a problem, particularly if the water is also poor in nutrients. Inserting a little barley straw is a good way of combatting this invader. When the straw begins to decompose, substances are released that kill algae, on the one hand, and, on the other hand, encourage healthy growth of water plants. Naturally, you cannot simply throw the barley straw into the pond. Take a handful and place it in a fist-sized gauze pouch that should be placed at the bottom of the trough, preferably weighted or covered with something. The effect will only be noticeable after a few weeks, when the straw starts decomposing, but may last up to nine months after that. In the transitional period, you should fish out larger colonies of algae with a stick or a fork. Recently, tablets made of decomposed straw have become available in the garden trade.

## Changing the water

Often, miniscule floating algae will cloud the water and may turn it grey, green, blueish or red. Once this clouding of the water has started (algae bloom), it would be a great mistake to change the water. The development of floating algae is connected with special environmental factors and is influenced by the nutrient content and temperature of the water, as well as by light conditions. All three of these factors change constantly during the course of the year, so this kind of algae bloom – by contrast to the insidious filamentous algae – will never last for very long.

Freshly created mini water gardens, in particular, often tend to form this type of algae. It would be completely wrong to change the water immediately, as the algae would recur quite rapidly. This algae bloom may recur for a short period every spring.

*Special attention must be given to the care of the water in your mini pond.*

### 'Vaccinating' the water

Should you wish to change the plants or the design of your mini pond, you might occasionally have to remove the water from the trough. You can use a hose to suck it into a drain. It is advisable to retain some of the water and put it aside for renewed use.

Then, when you fill up the trough again with fresh water, you can 'vaccinate' this fresh water with the saved water and vitalize it. In this way, biological equilibrium will soon be recreated in your mini pond.

# Care and overwintering

## Plant care in your mini pond

Plants have a natural urge to grow, flower and expand. Your mini pond will continue developing after its creation and, after just a few weeks, will present quite a different picture to that on the day of planting.

## Plants that form rhizomes

These plants should be watched more carefully. Some species expand so vigorously that they will, in time, become the dominant plant in the trough. The best way to keep this in check is to place all plants that form underground rhizomes inside a larger container which is then inserted into the trough. During the following summer, make sure that the rhizomes do not invade the rest of the trough by growing over the edge of their container. Always check these plants when you are checking the water level and, if necessary, snip off with your thumb nail any rhizomes that are escaping from their container.

## Repotting

This type of care will be necessary, at least every other year, for plants that form rhizomes. If not, the proliferating plants will fill their container to the point where they will no

*Both rushes and water mint form rhizomes and proliferate wildly.*

longer find any nutrients, and will push themselves up and out of their container with their rhizomes. At this point, at the very latest, take them out of their container and repot them. Use only a very few of the rhizomes of the old plant, and plant them in a fresh container. The best time for this task is spring, when the plant begins to shoot. The freshly repotted plant can then be put back in its old position.

## Dividing plants

Large herbaceous plants may, in time, develop into regular bushes. If they begin to look too big, they should be taken out and divided.

With some plants, you can simply break out a large piece or tear it off. Others require cutting the rootstock apart with a strong knife.

## Fertilizing

This is an area in which people tend to overdo things. An excessive supply of nutrients may lead to rapid algae formation. Once the plants in a trough have rooted well, and a micro-fauna has become established, a natural cycle is created. Plants and creatures die, sink to the bottom, and are broken down by bacteria and other micro-organisms. The breakdown products of this process provide plant-nourishing salts that are absorbed, in turn, by the plants' roots.

Only very fast-growing plants may occasionally suffer from lack of some nutrients and will remain smaller – in principle, a favourable state of affairs for the mini pond. You might poke half a fertilizer stick into the rootstock of one of these plants. In the case of water-lilies that do not grow a great deal, a small dose of phosphorous-rich fertilizer will encourage the development of flowers.

## Care of water-lilies

Water-lilies can be planted directly into the mini pond or inside a basket (see also pages 22–3). The specimens that have been planted straight into the bottom will be able to root all over the bottom of the container and will develop particularly well. To prevent them from spreading too much, reduce the plant every spring to only one short shoot with, at most, two side buds. Choose a vigorous shoot and remove the end of it plus all the other shoots. Water-lilies planted in baskets should be repotted after overwintering, taking care to remove all shoots except for the strongest. The exception are dwarf water-lilies. They grow so slowly that they require several years of undisturbed development in the same pot.

## Cutting plants

The growth and dying of plants are natural processes. Whether you decide to intervene or not is your own personal decision. On the one hand, dead shoots that decompose on the bottom bring fresh nutrients; on the other hand, dead plant parts will interfere with the appearance of your mini pond. Diseased leaves must definitely be removed, however, so they do not infect other plants. Only frog bit and mare's tail are susceptible. You will find reddish brown spots on the leaves of frog bit that will rapidly cover the whole leaf. If the damage spreads, you will need to cut out all the leaves. The plant will generally respond with vigorous new shoots. Mare's tail shoots may die above the surface of the water and should be removed immediately, cutting back to 1cm (⅜in) below the surface of the water. The plant should then produce healthy new growth.

## Fruits and seeds

Attractive autumnal fruit stands and dead grasses should not be cut back if the trough is left outside during the winter. They will present a charming picture with interesting silhouettes in winter, when they are covered with hoar frost or snow. The remaining dead parts of plants, that lie in the water or at the bottom of the trough, should be cut off and removed before the winter. You will also need to make sure that not too much organic matter is left in the water during the summer, or remains there later in the year.

# Care and overwintering

### Overwintering your mini pond

The choice of your plants (see page 21) and the material in which the containers and troughs for your mini water garden are made will determine whether they can remain outside during the winter, or whether the trough and some of the plants need to be kept in frost-free conditions in the house.

All indigenous marginal and water plants are hardy herbaceous plants, so they can be left outside without any qualms. They will not mind whether they are standing in containers or planted in troughs. This has been proven over many years in herbaceous plant nurseries. It also applies to plants that freeze up in the winter.

All troughs and bowls that can remain filled with water, because they have sloping sides, are ideal for overwintering outside. Indigenous plants in the marginal zone or moist zone, that grow above the surface of water, will not require any special protection, though covering them with conifer branches may provide a little extra protection.

All plant containers that will not resist the pressure build-up of freezing water either have to be emptied completely, or kept in a frost-free, preferably very bright room.

### A place for overwintering

The temperature in an overwintering place should not fall below 0°C (32°F) and should not rise above 5°C (41°F). Higher temperatures would cause the plants to begin shooting. If the position is not bright enough, they will suffer and die during the winter. The water will also evaporate quickly. During winter, the plants and their containers should never be allowed to dry out completely. You will need to check them regularly and top up the water.

### Non-hardy plants

These plants should be removed from the mini pond during the winter. Sensitivity to frost is indicated in the plant tables (see pages 14-15 and 18-19). Plants growing in individual containers are easily removed from the trough before the first frost, cleaned up, and stood in a watertight bowl or box in the kind of indoor conditions described above.

Frost-sensitive water-lilies require special handling. As a rule, they are planted in baskets, so they can be removed fairly easily from the mini pond. Immediately cut off all leaves on the rhizome, as well as all decaying parts. Then stand the water-lily in a bowl or bucket and fill it with water. The other option is to cover the plants with two fingers of moist peat.

### Overwintering troughs outside

Larger troughs that cannot be moved should remain outside and can be prepared for overwintering in situ. Troughs with vertical walls need draining, as the ice cannot expand upwards. Decayed or faded plant parts should be removed, so that decay does not take place over the winter. All hardy water-lilies and herbaceous plants can be left in the trough. To prevent them drying out through frost or winter sunshine, fill up the trough with dead leaves. Oak or beech leaves are recommended, as they do not decay easily due to their tannic acid content. The taller plants should be cut off, as you will need to cover up the trough to avoid it filling up with rainwater or snow. The best type of cover is transparent plastic or bubble pack. This will protect the trough from the most extreme temperatures. It will also allow light to penetrate, which is necessary for the plants.

*Indigenous marginal and water plants can be overwintered outside without suffering any harm.*

The plastic should not lie directly on top of the plants, but should be about 10cm (4in) above them. The air pocket created will have an insulating effect and will prevent the plants from decaying or being infested with moulds. You will need to fix the plastic firmly to the trough, so it does not fly off in winter gales. Even though troughs with sloping walls (see pages 38-9) are better for overwintering, they should also be covered with plastic.

## Overwintering pumps

If you have a pump for driving a fountain or similar (see pages 44-5) in your mini pond, you will have to switch it off and remove it in good time before the first frost, as pumps are very sensitive to frost and should be looked after with great care. Prevent the pump from drying out in the winter by storing it in a bucket of water in the overwintering room.

## The end of overwintering

At the beginning of the first month or the second month of spring, you can, as a rule, count on no more severe frosts. Now is the time to prepare the mini pond for summer. Troughs that have overwintered outside can have their covering of plastic or leaves removed now. Then, if necessary, repot the frost-sensitive plants (see pages 52-3) and put them back in their positions in the mini pond trough. Fill up the trough and containers with water again.

*During the summer months, the mini pond will unfold its beauty and splendour.*

## Care all year round

*Second and third months of winter* The troughs and small containers in the overwintering room need checking. Check water-lilies and other frost-sensitive plants in small containers to see whether they are still moist enough and add water, if necessary. Check the water levels and moisture of those containers standing outside, and check that any covering is secured properly.

*First month of spring* At the end of the month, when only light night frosts are expected, uncover the troughs standing outside, in order to harden the plants a little. Keep the covering material nearby, so it is readily to hand if there are severe late frosts.

*Second month of spring* Remove dead leaves from the troughs. Remove frost-sensitive plants from their overwintering place, repot if necessary, and place them back in their old positions in the troughs. Now make any alterations in the mini pond. Plants that have grown too large should be taken out, divided and a part replanted in the trough. Plants that you do not like any more should be removed and replaced by new ones in the last month of spring, Then fill the troughs and containers with water again.

*Last month of spring:* This is the season for water plants, as well as the best time to plant them or replace them. Now is the time you will find the greatest selection in garden centres and specialist nurseries. Check the pH value of the mini pond water and regulate it, if necessary.

*First month of summer* Check the water level. Cut back plants that are proliferating too wildly. Use a cone of flower fertilizer or a tablet of water plant fertilizer if your water-lilies have not started flowering. Use barley straw sacks if algae are forming.

*Second and third months of summer, first month of autumn* During the summer months, carefully monitor water levels and top up regularly. Occasionally check the pH value. Remove dead or diseased parts of plants.

*Second and third months of autumn* Plants are slowly beginning to die. Regularly remove decayed parts of plants that might rot during the winter. At the end of the last month of autumn, prepare the trough for the winter. Before the first severe frost, prepare frost-sensitive plants, along with non-frostproof containers and pumps, for overwintering inside.

*First month of winter* At the beginning of this month, at the latest, prepare troughs that are to remain outside and cover them for winterproofing. Now move non-frostproof containers and frost-sensitive plants to their overwintering quarters.

## Problem solving

Problems with your mini ponds will rarely occur, on the whole, and will not be disastrous. Problems with planting and with water will, as a rule, only occur if obvious mistakes have been made.

*Damage to the liner* Holes in PVC liners can be welded with hot air or welding agents – once you have removed the water. Repairing butyl liners is, however, rather more difficult. Smaller holes can be glued with transparent silicon glue. The liner will have to be completely dry and clean. The silicon glue is squirted onto the hole and smoothed flat to one side. In the middle of the silicon patch, exactly above the hole, apply the mass more thickly. Then, allow the silicon mass to dry for half a day and set, before letting water back in. If the damage is more extensive, you will need to replace the liner altogether.

*Loss of water* If you notice water is leaking away from the start, and there is no hole, check whether one of the folds behind the liner has slipped away downwards. The corner of the liner should be continuously visible along the edge of the trough.

# Index

# Index

# Acknowledgements

## Sources

Plant containers and technical accessories for your mini pond can be obtained through most large garden centres, especially those that specialize in water plants and herbaceous plants, as well as from suppliers of ponds and pond equipment.

## Photographic acknowledgements

The photos in this volume are by Friedrich Strauss, with the exception of the following:
A–Z Botanical Collection Ltd: front cover, top and bottom insets;
Flora/Casperson page 28;
The Garden Picture Library: front cover, middle inset;
Gräfe und Unzer Verlag GmbH: front cover, main picture;
IPO/Polaschek: C1 (small photo);
mein schöner Garten/Fischer: pages 2, 17 top, C4 bottom;
Reinhard: pages 13 centre left, 16 bottom left, bottom right;
Sammer: pages 33
Schimana: pages 3 left, 55, C4 top right;
Stehling: pages 21, 31, 52;
Stork: page 39;
Tschakert: page 8

## Acknowledgements

The publishers and the author wish to thank Hans-Jürgen Goetzke of the Munich Botanical Gardens for expert advice, and for proofreading the manuscript. Further thanks go to the employees of the garden centre Pflanzen Kölle, Munich, and to Christiane Widmayr-Falconi of the Gartengalerie, Murnau, Staffelsee, for their support.

## Author's notes

This volume deals with the planting and care of water plants. Some of the plants described are toxic. They have been indicated by a death's head symbol on pages 18–19. Make absolutely sure that children and pets do not consume the plants marked as dangerous. Special care should be taken that the skin-irritating, milky sap in the Euphorbia species does not get into anyone's eyes.

Some of the chapters (pages 42–3 and 44–5) discuss lighting your mini pond, as well as using an electric pump to drive fountains. Remember that any kind of electrical installations should be carried out by an expert, for safety reasons. Making connections to a power source, as well as running cables outside, belong in this category. When installing one or more mini ponds on your balcony or patio, remember to consult any tenancy or other agreements (leasehold), but also make sure that you check the weight-bearing capacity of the balcony or patio. Every mini pond owner needs to ensure that no water can run over onto the balcony, patio or into a neighbouring apartment. Regularly check the mini pond, as well as any water connections outside, and take proper precautions when changing water or emptying troughs (see pages 8–9).

## Cover photographs

Front cover: main picture, wooden barrel pond with water-lilies; top inset, water crowfoot; middle inset, purple loosestrife; bottom inset, water forget-me-not.
Back cover: water-lily,

This edition published 2001
Murdoch Books UK Ltd
Ferry House, 51-57 Lacy Road,
Putney, London SW15 1PR

ISBN 1–85391–955 1

© 1996 Gräfe & Unzer Verlag GmbH, Munich.

English text copyright © Murdoch Books UK Ltd 2000
Translated by Astrid Mick
Typesetting and editorial by Grapevine Publishing Services Ltd
Printed in Hong Kong by Wing King Tong

# Water casts a spell on the patio

Most of us are drawn to water as if by magic, as this element of life has a strong influence on our senses. You begin to feel calm and happy beside water, as everyday cares become unimportant. This world of water can be experienced in the smallest spaces – as here, with this attractively combined mini pond arrangement on a patio. Green plants thrive and bloom in rustic wooden barrels, and a small fountain in the background brings a lively element into the scene.

*The little water-lily pond in the tub is framed by varied, attractively planted, wooden tubs of varying heights.*